the friendship diet

CLEAN OUT YOUR FRIDGE, GET REAL
WITH YOURSELF, AND FILL YOUR LIFE WITH
MEANINGFUL RELATIONSHIPS THAT LAST

SHERI JACOBS

Publishing services provided by **Archangel Ink**

ISBN: 978-1-950043-10-1

Four Steps to Conquering Your Comfort Zone Diet

Before you begin reading this book, I have a free bonus to offer you.

In addition to the information already provided in this book, I created an audio guide called *Four Steps to Conquering Your Comfort Zone Diet*.

This simple but challenging plan will catapult you out of an unhealthy relationship diet and into a rewarding and nutrient-rich one.

To receive your free bonus, simply sign up for my mailing list at:

www.sheri-jacobs.com/book-bonus

By subscribing, you'll also be notified of any pending book releases or updated content, and you'll get to be first in line for exclusive deals and future book giveaways.

Immediately after signing up, you'll be sent an email with access to the bonus—both the audio and PDF version of my *Four Steps to Conquering Your Comfort Zone Diet*!

Sheri Jacobs

Acknowledgments

My heartfelt thanks to the following people for their wisdom, assistance, and dedication to make this book a reality: Jordan Ring, Kristie Lynn, and Rob Archangel—you are all literary angels and a joy to work with.

Thank you to Paige Duke, editor extraordinaire! Your laser focus and insight are mesmerizing to witness.

Thank you to my dear friend and maven of words and stories, Cathey Nickell. The seed for this book may have formed from the unknown synergy between experience and thought, but your "Be Amazing" support and insight caused that seed to grow. Your can-do attitude is wonderfully contagious and makes my heart swell with gratitude.

Thank you to Barry Ruback for cheering me on from those first embryonic drafts. Your unwavering faith in this book and in me is palpable.

Thank you to Ricardo Rivadeneira for your genuine feedback. Your passion for the book's journey means the world to me.

Thank you to Fran and Joel Jacobs: my parents, my teachers, and my spiritual cheerleaders.

Thank you to Cindy Weinstein and Tara Mauer for always having my back.

To all the brave hearts that want to know their hunger.

Contents

Introduction:
Why the Friendship Diet?

*Insanity: doing the same thing over and over again
and expecting different results.*
—Albert Einstein

I magine a monkey in a tree (male or female works, but for the purposes of this story, let's pick one gender), enjoying her banana (you can interpret the object in this sentence any way you like…). But she drops her banana mid-munch. Instead of missing that banana, instead of wondering why the banana fell or why she even chose "that" banana, she is suddenly hungry to fill the void of her empty paws with another banana.

And so, our furry heroine jumps to the next tree and grabs the nearest available banana. She doesn't take the time to discern the sizes of the different bananas (if you take that as a pun, so be it—I cannot control where your mind goes ☺) around her, doesn't even notice the dark spots dotting the yellow exterior. She is so hungry to fill herself up with something—fast—that she may as well be blindfolded as she eagerly shoves the next banana into her mouth.

Unfortunately, in our monkey's haste to self-satiate, she neglects to notice the fire ants climbing from the tree onto her buttocks. It is the pain that wakes her from her eating frenzy. Sharp, electrical sparks course through our monkey's veins. The pain is too much; she falls, plummeting to the rocky earth below.

Yet despite her intense convulsions of pain, despite the fact that her legs are bruised (and possibly fractured) from her fall, our opposable-thumbed gal picks up the now slimy, dirt-covered half-eaten banana and puts it into her mouth. She is aware of how nasty it tastes but rationalizes *she's hungry and needs to eat SOMEONE*—er, something.

When she is finished, our frustrated gal realizes she's still pining for something, still feeling an inexplicable void. So she does what she always does: she staggers for the nearest NEXT banana (that fall did a number on her) hanging from a tree within her furry arm's reach. Deep down, she doesn't even want the banana; deep down, she would much prefer to take a nap or read a good book. (She's a smart monkey.) But eating bananas is all she knows.

When our monkey goes to pluck the next banana (an overly ripe one with smashed insides), an aggressive fellow monkey (with major self-esteem issues and a competitive personality) snags the banana right out of our heroine's hands.

Tabatha (what—you didn't think I'd give her a name?) watches, heartbroken as *her* banana goes off into the sunset with the furry bitch (who needs some serious waxing). She is so consumed with this idea that *someone took her banana* that she doesn't allow herself to consider:

1. She didn't even know the banana.
2. Deep down, she didn't even want the banana.
3. She needs to see a doctor for those nasty fire ant bites and the massive swelling of her apparently broken legs (it was a long fall).

Poor Tabatha is so immersed in self-pity and that constant need to fill her inexplicable void that she doesn't even notice the world around her. She doesn't see the jungle is filled with much more than bananas. Hyper-focused on finding the right banana, Tabatha doesn't even realize that she is really a mango girl (and there are plenty of mangoes in the jungle).

*****

If you are reading this book, chances are you are not very different from Tabatha. I know I wasn't. Serial monogamy was my comfort food. I swung from one serious relationship to the next, never giving myself the gift of time: time to know myself a little better, time to ask questions and really listen to the answers, time to notice what I liked and didn't like, time to reflect on what mattered to me. From the time I was aware of the many "bananas" out there (we're talking kindergarten—Michael Marcotrigiano, my first crush), I unconsciously chose to focus my attention on boys, then men, altering myself to gain their attention. Had I gone inward instead of outward for approval, the landscape of my life and its trajectory would look vastly different today.

My hunger for figurative bananas caused me to contort myself to fit what "they" wanted so that I never received the gift of knowing myself. Boyfriends became husbands because I HAD to be with someone; reflecting on my past relationships was too daunting—it was much easier to grab the next fruit nearby. I married someone who reflected who I was in my early twenties: desperate for love and looking anywhere but within for acceptance and approval. When two people are starving for emotional nutrition and looking externally to fill the void of self-worth, it's a recipe for disaster. Unfortunately, the beautiful soul of my husband left this earth before he could alter his perspective.

When my second marriage ended, Albert Einstein's famous quote percolated in my mind: "Insanity is doing the same thing over and over again and expecting different results." I was forty-two and divorced, determined to no longer accept the norm of my life. It was time for me to stop the insanity of constant monogamy and go inward instead of looking outward for happiness.

Did I want to date? Did I want to enjoy the company of another man? ABSOLUTELY! I was craving companionship the way I craved the Ben & Jerry's ice cream in the frozen food aisle. But this time was different. This time, I was going to fight temptation. I refused to jump into a relationship just to satisfy my old yearning to have a Someone.

I wrote this book because of that brilliant Einstein quote and the eureka effect it had on me after my divorce in 2015. Our most personal relationships are like food: they possess the potential to starve or feed our souls. And the most important source of sustenance is the relationship we have with ourselves. Until we get to know ourselves, we are potentially digesting nutritionally weak fare.

Comfort food comes in all different flavors: serial one-night stands, serial seclusion, serial emotional distancing, serial affairs. Bottom line, if it's something you find yourself doing for extended periods of time, chances are you're emotionally and spiritually dwelling in a comfort zone. And there's nothing wrong with this if you are satiated, fulfilled, dare I say happy.

But if you were in a "good place," you wouldn't be reading these words now. And if I were satiated, I wouldn't have embarked on writing this book! Whatever your sexual orientation or gender identity, whether you have been married to the same person you lost your virginity to and suddenly find yourself on your own or you are recently divorced and terrified to date, you my friend, are Tabatha.

Tabatha, while a fictionalized female monkey, is all of us. She is living a life sans self-reflection, ignoring or disregarding what she feels and unaware of the wonderful possibilities around and within her.

The Friendship Diet is an emotional and spiritual fitness plan to feed ourselves nutritious relationships, to catapult ourselves out of the psychological ruts we have plowed from years of living in our respective comfort zones, and to feel satiated again.

The "prescription" for the Friendship Diet is different for everyone. After all, a serial commitment-phobe is going to require a plan that looks nothing like that of the serial monogamist. Yet all of our challenges share one common denominator: living in our comfort zone.

I invite you to join me in embarking on something new. Let's go off the beaten path and try to feed ourselves a diet that is jam-packed with relationship nutrition, anathema to what twenty-first century society considers "normal."

Here's what I've garnered during my four-plus decades living as a female *Homo sapiens* on our beloved planet Earth: two major events need to occur in order to create a shift or change:

1. Reflection
2. Action

So as you read this book, question the heck out of my words. Take the time to digest the thoughts, perspectives, and observations offered throughout the Have-I-No-Shame (nay, I do not) attempts to compare intimate relationships to food. If a string of words hits you a certain way, acknowledge it, observe it, *reflect* on what this might mean for you. Typically, when a chord is struck or a nerve is hit, there's something needing your attention.

To make life easier for you (I'm all about convenience), I've included a short opportunity for reflection after each chapter to encourage you to delve further into any potential epiphanies or "Hmmm…" moments. You may want to use a nice journal to expand on these reflective opportunities—after all, this Friendship Diet starts and ends with the most important relationship you will ever have: the one with yourself! So it makes perfect sense that you might find yourself considering a Moleskine journal or a plain diary just itching to be bedazzled (but I digress…). No need to go out and buy something, though. You can scribble your thoughts on last week's grocery list, if you wish. What you write on doesn't matter—the key is to create momentum. When we reflect and take the time to physically articulate the jumble of emotions and awakenings percolating through our hearts and minds, something magical occurs: the kinesthetic act of writing creates a shift. The *action* of writing creates change.

As a single mom and teacher, I know full well that you may disregard the whole mini-reflection effort as pointless. Maybe you're already rolling your eyes at me. (Is it that obvious I teach writing to teenagers? Don't answer that.)

But I'm telling you, writing is where the magic, the light-bulb moment, the clarity occurs.

One last but necessary note: there will be times when you are ready to throw in the towel. You'll know this because you will either feel: A) This is stupid, or B) I don't have time for this Oprah-esque literary babble.

When the above scoffing or potential sarcasm occurs, know that means you are very likely about to break out of your comfort zone, out of the psychic grooves that are no longer serving you. The closer we get to the source of our broken heart, the more desperately we want to avoid seeing it.

Remember: there's a reason you picked up this book. Be brave. When you want to give up, go *in*. It's the only way through to the healthy intimate relationships we all deserve.

Happy-Meal Dating

When someone shows you who they are,
believe them the first time.
–Maya Angelou

I used to think the worst thing in life was to end up
all alone. It's not. The worst thing in life is to end
up with people that make you feel all alone.
–Robin Williams

Don't let someone change who you are
to become what they need.
–Anonymous

Burger King, McDonald's, Wendy's. There's a whole slew of fast food chains that offer a tissue-wrapped assortment of edible cuteness—complete with a toy! As a kid, I LIVED for Friday: the one day of the week my mother would grant me the coveted Burger King Kids Meal. It didn't matter that there was no healthy food within the flimsy cardboard mini-house, that there was perhaps more nutrition to be found in my little sister's Play-Doh set. It was the aesthetics of that tiny burger wrapped up in that circa-1970 colored tissue paper (despite the fact that it was the eighties), the adorable white paper bag holding the (greasy) fries, and oh (drumroll, please), the mysterious toy I was itching to rip open and play with.

But here was the reality: eating that crap left me with heartburn and stomach pain. The Made-in-Some-Factory-with-Toxic-Materials "toy" almost always fell apart within minutes and/or was nothing more than a mirage of fun—in truth, it was absolutely boring.

When we date the wrong person for us or we stay in a relationship that doesn't serve us, we are Happy-Meal Dating: filling our hearts and minds with crap. We aren't providing ourselves the proper nutrition we need to feel good and grow spiritually. We remain stagnant, perhaps weak and even sick.

Remember that brave soul, director Morgan Spurlock? He is the courageous dude who studied the effects of McDonald's foods on the body, using his poor self as the guinea pig. For an entire month, Spurlock subsisted solely on McDonald's. The results, which he documented in his brilliant 2004 documentary *Super Size Me*, were frightening (though, let's be honest, not too surprising).

Spurlock's weight ballooned, his energy crashed (he even had trouble getting his "banana" up…), his cholesterol level rose to unprecedented levels, and his liver looked like that of an alcoholic.

No, I am not saying that when we date we are creating a recipe for obesity and impotence. I am saying that when we continue to go for the surface of things, chronically chase the shiny new relationship, and neglect to take time to get to know what's going on under the other person's "Happy Meal," we are doing ourselves a disservice.

Happy-Meal Dating can manifest all kinds of sugar-coated, ego-driven, sparkly toxins. An old friend dated the man who would become her husband because he was a police officer, and she found something sexy about the whole man-in-uniform thing. She also loved the perks that came with dating a man of the law: free tickets to sold-out concerts, celebrity meetings behind the scenes, and coveted seats to an Astros game, to name a few. She didn't care for the verbal abuse hurled at her behind closed doors. Still, the lure of the uniform and its advantages made walking away that much harder.

It is a couple of decades later and despite the two beautiful girls they have and the marriage still legal on paper, my now former friend has had an ongoing intermittent affair with someone from her high school days. It was one thing when my friend decided to marry a man for the image of his uniform and all the perks that came with it, but when she started a hidden relationship with another man, *I* couldn't digest being around her. And perhaps she experiences moments of happiness during her clandestine rendezvous, but on a soul level, she's living a nutritionally toxic life. Unfortunately, that toxicity is ingested—even on a subconscious level—by her husband and children.

Journal Time

What shiny, sparkly, ego-driven "Happy Meals" attract you? Keep in mind that the decadence of these highly caloric foods can prevent us from seeing that this person is a nutritional disaster for us.[1]

My Happy-Meal-sparkly-shiny-ego-driven turn-ons:

_____

_____

_____

_____

_____

_____

_____

_____

_____

_____

---

1   Remember: The more reflective and real you can be with these exercises, the greater the possibility of leaving your comfort zone(s) and experiencing authentic, rewarding relationships.

Recognizing When There's a Bar of Soap in Your Mouth

Wanting things for the wrong reasons can turn anyone's life into a marshmallow on a stick over a hot fire: impossibly messy and eventually consumed, one way or another.
—Deb Caletti

I reside in Texas, where cilantro is the omnipresent herb of choice. Considering it's also known as Mexican parsley, it's no surprise that the popular seasoning found a welcome home in the Southwest. My older sister drools each time she visits me from her New Jersey home, adorning her Tex-Mex enchiladas with generous splashes of the freshly torn green leaves. My colleagues think nothing of digging into homemade guacamole with the verdant specks of cilantro proudly poking through the avocado-based dip.

Alas, for me, cilantro tastes like soap. Seriously, if someone stuffed a bar of Dial in my mouth, I would consider it a solidified larger version of the green plant.

Yet for years I tried to force myself to eat everything from tortillas to gazpacho with the pretty green flakes sprinkled on top. Why? Here's my sad little defense:

1. I was a native New Yorker, so the Mexican parsley didn't make its appearance on my plate too often.
2. Whenever I declined cilantro, I received looks of shock, confusion, and borderline distrust not altogether different from the expression one might make when finding out a person dresses up her cat and photographs it to make photo calendars.

3. I badly wanted to fit in. I didn't want to seem high maintenance to my peers or the restaurant staff.

So I ignored the soapy taste for years until a gentleman at a local Freebirds kindly informed me that the soapy taste is a by-product of genetics. Suddenly, my taste buds, my gustatory perception, were validated!

Yes, I'm aware of how sad it is that a stranger's undocumented genetic wisdom regarding the ubiquitous parsley was the only thing granting me permission to finally feel justified, normal. No longer was I the strange gal who dressed up cats for her annual photo calendar; I was just an ordinary woman, genetically programmed to taste soap while ingesting cilantro.

According to *Huffington Post* author Carly Ledbetter, only about 4–14% of the population experiences the soapy taste when eating cilantro. "Scientists were able to pin down most cilantro haters as people with a shared group of olfactory-receptor genes, called OR6A2, that pick up on the smell of aldehyde chemicals. Aldehyde chemicals are found in both cilantro *and* soap."[2]

So not only is the soapy taste of cilantro normal, but I experience the Ivory Snow flavor each time it's in my mouth because my sense of smell is so advanced!

We all have the Bar-of-Soap-in-the-Mouth (BSM) experience at one point or another in our intimate relationships. Sometimes it's subtle, sometimes it's visceral, but recognizing and acknowledging it is vital.

---

2   Carly Ledbetter, "Science Explains Why Cilantro Tastes Like Soap for Certain People," *The Huffington Post*, December 6, 2017, https://www.huffpost.com/entry/why-does-cilantro-taste-bad-like -soap_n_7653808.

I have a friend whose BSM is recurring stomach pain after a night out with her husband. It has nothing to do with the food and everything to do with the layers of Spanx she wears, insisting that she needs to suck in her midsection in order for hubby to find her attractive. She waits until he's in the shower to remove her Lycra torture chamber and bides her time until he's sleeping to sneak downstairs to the kitchen, where she can finally eat in her blessedly forgiving pajama pants.

Now, there's nothing wrong with sporting a pair of Spanx, but there is an issue with perpetual self-induced abdominal pain concealed from a spouse in an effort to be considered thin enough. There is a problem with holding said aching-to-be-released belly in Lycra until said husband is out of sight. There is a blazing red flag when a woman feels she cannot partake in gustatory pleasure around her own husband.

There is nothing wrong with wanting to look aesthetically pleasing to our partners, but it shouldn't come at the cost of abdominal pain. My friend's Spanx-bandaged midsection is her BSM. It is a symbol of something systemic in their relationship that needs addressing, not much different than my literal BSM, which was more about low self-esteem than a harmless green leaf. It may well be that my friend's self-induced torture stems from her poor body image and that her husband bears no influence in her decision to suffer. Regardless of her motivation, my friend's BSM causes physical pain.

Recognizing our own BSM is about acknowledging what works and doesn't work for us. That sounds easy enough, yet when we throw society (e.g., parental expectations, family customs, and people pleasing) into the psychological mix, we can easily put our own BSMs on the backburner in order to please or win the approval of others.

No matter your gender identity, age, or sexual orientation, you've probably experienced the temptation to ignore the turnoffs or unhealthy behaviors of others in order to satisfy their expectations. Often we may not even realize we are doing this except in hindsight.

When I was nineteen, my sister set me up with a twenty-four-year-old coworker. He was the "right" religion for my mother, and it didn't hurt that the guy brought her ice cream on our first date. One half-gallon of Dairy Queen and my mom was smitten.

Unfortunately, I didn't see the same man she did. Matt was one of those loud guys who laughed a little too hard at his own jokes. When he wasn't ass-kissing my mother, his hands seemed to multiply, his sausage-like fingers poking me from all angles. True, he wasn't cilantro, but I still experienced the BSM in the form of his personality.

Still, I agreed to go out with Matt. Ignoring my reservations, I allowed him to drive me back to his apartment. Let's just say I felt like Penelope (remember the reluctant love interest of Pepé Le Pew?), and in the end, a very angry and sexually frustrated Matt drove me home.

Had I heeded my inner compass, not one of Matt's sausage fingers would have ever touched my skin. The fact that I was nineteen is no excuse—listening to that inner voice, knowing when you are experiencing a BSM in a relationship is available to us at any age and at any moment. The founder of philosophical Taoism, Lao Tzu, reminds us,

"The journey of a thousand miles begins with one step."[3] To alter our tendency to heed the familiar, we can consciously choose to slow down and listen to that internal compass, one moment and—with time—one action at a time.

The Friendship Diet is an opportunity to nourish yourself by hitting the pause button on outside influences. It's a reminder that your opinion of yourself is what matters most; it's your time to stop binge eating all of the psychological crap food that well-meaning (and sometimes not so well-meaning) significant others keep dishing. It's a call for self-reflection and, by extension, an invitation to grow.

---

3   "Lao Tzu Quotes," Brainy Quote, accessed November 19, 2019, https://www.brainyquote.com/quotes/lao_tzu_137141.

Journal Time

Are you sick of strappy sandals that leave burn marks on your instep? Or something more serious, like the alcohol your partner orders for you when he knows you are trying to give up the stuff? Compromise is one thing, but ignoring how you feel about something is no different than my self-destructive habit of eating a fajita covered in cilantro and pretending it tastes like anything other than a Bath & Body Works product.

Take a moment to consider your own BSM blind spots. We can't expect to speak up if we don't first identify the conflict—both inside ourselves and within our intimate relationships.

My Bar-of-Soap-in-the-Mouth blind spots:

_____

_____

_____

_____

_____

_____

_____

_____

What could/might happen if I articulated/acknowledged my Bar-of-Soap-in-the-Mouth experiences?

_____

_____

_____

_____

_____

_____

_____

_____

_____

_____

_____

_____

_____

Identifying Empty Calories

*The best day of your life is the one on which you decide
your life is your own. No apologies or excuses. No one
to lean on, rely on, or blame. The gift is yours—it is an
amazing journey—and you alone are responsible for the
quality of it. This is the day your life really begins.*
—Bob Moawad

What's one of the worst things we can do on an empty, growling stomach? Enter a supermarket, of course. With a satiated tummy, we can make wise choices, choosing the fresh produce over the potato chips. But if we dare venture into a grocery store with a belly devoid of nutrients, we're likely to make some physically and financially expensive mistakes.

With a full belly, we're happy to pick up the organic olive oil and vibrant steak tomatoes. The kale and avocadoes look appetizing and pop right into our shopping carts, along with the crisp apples and vitamin-packed kiwis. Our eyes don't even register the plastic-sealed chips and shiny cookie wrappers in the snack aisles. No, sir, with a full belly, we can glide through the supermarket with confidence and ease, knowing we are making good nutritional choices.

An empty tummy will only bring you great caloric trouble. Walking through that same supermarket with a growling, unsatisfied feeling in our stomachs, we morph into self-rationalizing creatures who drool over the same "delights" pumped full of high-fructose corn syrup and wrapped in cellophane that we ignored in our satiated state.

Grocery shopping, dining out, or even attending a swanky soiree—the occasion doesn't matter if hunger is involved. Hunger has a life force of its own. An incredible amount of self-control is needed to navigate past a caloric landmine into the pragmatic terrain of fruits and vegetables.

Relationships are like that: we need to feed ourselves healthy relationships in order to stave off poor or even toxic company.

When it comes to relationships, loneliness is the emotional equivalent of hunger. We can sometimes become so starved for connection and company that we fill ourselves up with bad company or company that is not beneficial to our emotional, physical, or spiritual growth.

It's a lot like how we know deep down as we pass those potato chips that look so pretty all lined up in their cans, begging for us to devour them, that we are going to feel worse, not better, after eating a bunch of salt and grease.

Journal Time

Take a moment to reflect on the people in your life you consider the human equivalent of "empty calories." These are the people who leave you feeling *less* energetic; these are the emotional "cookies and cakes" that may give you a quick rush of something that feels good temporarily but render you depleted in some way shortly thereafter.

Either in the space below or in that sticker-covered Lisa Frank journal you have created for the Friendship Diet, write what your life might be like if you didn't spend your free time in this person's/these people's company. Pay attention to any fear or anxiety that comes up during this exercise. This kind of resistance is normal when you start challenging yourself, poking the sleeping bear of Comfort. I ask you: Would it be any easier to give up your favorite junk food? Of course not. Yet you know that on the other side of your resistance is opportunity, a chance for you to morph from a state of hunger into one of satisfaction.

Identifying your empty calories is the first step on the road to an emotionally healthy diet.

Empty-calorie companions:

_____

_____

_____

_____

_____

_____

_____

_____

_____

_____

_____

_____

_____

My life without the close company of empty-calorie companions:

_____

_____

_____

_____

_____

_____

_____

_____

_____

_____

_____

_____

_____

_____

_____

What's in Your Kitchen?

*What lies behind us and what lies before us are
tiny matters compared to what lies within us.*
–Ralph Waldo Emerson

*Sometimes it takes a heartbreak to shake us awake and help
us see we are worth so much more than we're settling for.*
–Mandy Hale, *The Single Woman: Life, Love, and a Dash of Sass*

When a relationship ends, there is the inevitable emotional terrain that needs to be considered. Sure, we can ignore it and shove it in the back with the rest of the psychological debris we've accumulated from living on planet Earth as a human. Yet there's a price for avoiding what needs to happen.

You ever ignore the leftover deli meat that went bad? Ever forget to empty that Tupperware of vegetables from last month and return to find the blue-hued mold growing on what used to be cauliflower? You begrudgingly don a pair of impenetrable gloves and pinch your nose to throw said rotting-memory-of-veggies in the trash, mentally promising to take the trash to the curb.

In one form or another, we've all done it: delayed the inevitable emptying of the trash, ignored the bevy of fungus growing in the fridge, mourned the stalactites and stalagmites of metallic-tasting ice-coated ice cream (yes, I've tried it—not my proudest moment) that is long past its creamy prime. And in one manifestation or another, we've all come face to face with the various costs involved with our kitchen delays.

But what happens when we keep our gloves on and start emptying our fridges and freezers? What happens when we go through our kitchen pantries to face the nutritional truth of what is waiting inside?

In my own experience, sifting and sorting through my kitchen feels an awful lot like excavating the topography of a broken heart: there's the denial (it can't be THAT bad, can it?), the excuses (I can't deal with this now; maybe next week I'll be in a better place to handle this mess…), the fear of the unknown (what will I find when I look inside?), and let's not forget the moments of disgust and anger—commonly referred to as the Blame Game (This would still be good if "someone else" hadn't [fill in the blank]!)

But something magical happens if we are willing to really "get in there" and examine what we've been hungry to avoid. We start to see our kitchens from a different perspective. Once the chicken teriyaki from three weeks ago and the circa-1995 barbeque sauce have been removed, once a healthy dose of Bon Ami is poured onto those stubborn dried eggshells from last year, once the wine stain from a decade ago has been erased by Mr. Clean, the world seems to be much more manageable, more logical. Suddenly, you have a brand-new fridge. Suddenly you feel as if you have all the space in the world and life is just beginning for you. And hey, bonus: you discover a brand-new six pack of sparkling water in the back of that fridge! Go YOU!

Breakups are a lot like a neglected kitchen: if we don't examine what went wrong or what parts of it "spoiled," we are more likely to continue filling our metaphorical fridges (relationships) with similar patterns.

Relationships are always teaching us; we just need to be ready to hear the lesson(s). Romantic relationships, since they are typically the most intimate, often teach us the biggest lessons. When my thirteen-year relationship ended, I wanted nothing more than to run out and fill my metaphorical fridge with new "produce." But instead, I took the time to excavate the emotional terrain of my broken heart. I stared, screamed, laughed, and cried until I had no more tears for our relationship, stretched long past its expiration date. Cleaning my relational fridge took a good few years. And now my "kitchen" feels expansive. My perspective has changed since I first started looking inside my pantry, with the spilled salt and stale Cheerios hiding behind the recycling bin.

Journal Time

Take a moment to consider a broken relationship from your life, past or present. What did or doesn't work anymore? Why? Face your inner "fridge" and "pantry." It will tell you volumes both about yourself and why the relationship doesn't or didn't work.

My broken relationship:

_____

_____

_____

_____

_____

_____

_____

_____

_____

_____

_____

Why the relationship doesn't/didn't work:

_____

_____

_____

_____

_____

_____

_____

_____

_____

_____

_____

_____

_____

Excavating this broken relationship is a process.
I now feel:

_____

_____

_____

_____

_____

_____

_____

_____

_____

_____

_____

_____

_____

_____

After examining/exploring/cleaning out my metaphorical kitchen, I feel:

_____

_____

_____

_____

_____

_____

_____

_____

_____

_____

_____

_____

_____

Irrational Nutrition

Nothing defines humans better than their
willingness to do irrational things in the pursuit
of phenomenally unlikely payoffs. This is the
principle behind lotteries, dating, and religion.
—Scott Adams

T he other day during a quick lunch break, I overheard
the following dialogue:

"I'm going out with that guy again tonight." Cue blush-
ing cheeks and a playful smile.

"Have you had sex with him yet?" a fellow colleague
inquires, looking up from her smartphone.

"No." A deeper blush ensues.

"Well, what are you waiting for, hon? How many times
you been out with this man?"

"This will be our third time."

"Three-date rule," another colleague quips before
downing her Dr. Pepper.

"That's right—three dates and you *gotta* hook up,"
adds the first colleague without looking up from her
smartphone.

"Uh, okay." The girl giggles and flashes a fearfully tight
smile.

To clarify: I do not work in a prison system or some
sketchy illegal and underground drug world. I am a public
school teacher. Yup. This conversation took place among
college-educated women who devote a great portion of

their lives striving to educate and help children. Two of them are mothers themselves. They are attractive, funny, and compassionate. They are also unaware of how amazing they are.

And yet…without realizing it, these women are sabotaging themselves and selling themselves short. I mean, *come on*! I might expect to hear a conversation like this among women who just came from a bar fight or college girls acting out of low self-esteem and ignoring unaddressed daddy issues.

And yet, each of my colleagues runs her classroom like a tight ship with an awesome mixture of compassion and discipline, challenging her students yet not overwhelming them, supporting students without enabling them.

Clearly, they have yet to discover their awesomeness. They are, whether consciously or unconsciously, allowing the unspoken "rules" of dating and society to dictate when a woman's physical intimacy with another "requires" commencement.

I had to exercise a great deal of self-control not to slap each of these amazing women silly until they woke up from their blind acceptance of the Asinine Rules of Dating (ARODs).

The ARODs are purely and simply asinine because society has no business dictating what works and doesn't work for an individual. The moment we surrender to society's expectation(s) of what is or isn't appropriate for consenting adults to do or not do in the bedroom is the moment we lose ourselves; that's the moment we begin to lie to ourselves.

ARODs are dangerous because they put your heart, mind, and soul on autopilot. You are no longer thinking for yourself; you are trusting the memes of the dating world instead of your inner world.

What was the point of cleaning out your kitchen if you're only going to fill it with the nutritional desires and needs of others?

Listen, if your best friend is a diabetic and you're lactose intolerant, are you going to order a cup of the sugar-free frozen yogurt she swears by? And will you be pushing her to try the dairy-free Twizzlers you absolutely love?

The answer is a resounding "Hell no!" when it comes to food, yet somehow the nuances of our emotional, physical, and spiritual needs are rarely considered. Our culture perpetuates one-size-fits-all advice for intimate relationships. Here are some stealthy ARODs lurking around our twenty-first-century world:

The man always pays.

He needs to make X amount of money.

For men to determine the "right" age of their dating partners, divide your age by two and then add seven.

He drives an old/inexpensive/unattractive car. I don't think so.

A boob job will attract a wealthy man.

The key is to find yourself a rich man/woman.

The key is to find someone who loves you more than you love him.

Make him think you care what he thinks and then do whatever you want.

Whatever you do, DON'T have sex until (insert AROD designated time).

You should have sex before (insert alternate AROD time here) if you want to keep him.

Buy her expensive things and then do whatever you want.[4,5]

As it happens, my conscience got the best of me (I could see the peer pressure all over my colleague's tomato-red face), and I had a little heart-to-heart with her privately.

"You know you don't need to have sex with this new guy you like unless you're ready and want to," I said.

"I'm so glad you said something. I really am not ready to, but I know that's what everyone expects."

"Who's everyone?"

My colleague played with a wayward strand on her shirt, unwilling or unable to make eye contact. "It's just that I'm not ready, you know?"

"So don't."

She just shrugged her shoulders and gave me a tight smile. "I need to make some photocopies."

Notice my colleague couldn't even name/identify who "everyone" is. That's because the ARODs are created by hundreds—no, thousands—of people from all walks of life, offering prescriptive nutritional advice on dating that may have worked for SOME people. The danger is thinking the ARODs are meant for every single soul. The danger is accepting an AROD in the first place. The danger is the unconscious digestion of ARODs.

By her tomato-red cheeks and her incessant playing with the flyaway string on her shirt, I could clearly see my

---

4   The above list can be applied—in most cases—to both genders.

5   The above list can, sadly, go on *ad nauseam*.

colleague was ingesting the AROD diet and growing sicker by the moment.

Before my forties, I was unconscious of the ARODs lurking around society. In my twenties, I chronically ingested ARODs such as:

> *Don't call him first. Let him come to you.*
> *Let him know you like him, but don't seem "too" interested.*
> *If he asks you out for that day, make him wait or else he'll think you're desperate.*
> *Don't pick up on the first ring. You'll seem too eager. (Remember, it was the nineties—no texting existed way back when.)*[6]

The other day, a dear friend of mine said, "Sheri, whoever you date now, make sure he has money. You need to be taken care of at this stage in your life."

The advice, like a pill that goes down the wrong pipe and is still bothering my esophagus two hours later, left an uncomfortable sensation in my body. Had I been in my twenties or even thirties, I probably would have just pushed the discomfort away by getting busy doing something else instead of pausing to examine the "why" behind my discomfort.

Instead, I sat with my friend's well-meaning advice and realized that was her nutritional prescription, not mine. What had created the uncomfortable sensation in my body was swallowing *her* belief, *her* prescribed diet.

Her belief, in my eyes, was an AROD—for ME. For over thirteen years, I had lived on an affluent diet of material riches that left my soul starving. There is nothing wrong

---

6   Again, I can go on. But you get the idea.

with money—it is neither good nor bad, after all. Money is nothing more than another form of energy, and it is what we do with that energy that matters.

Yet the prescribed notion that money is the required prerequisite to a romantic partnership stirred up a sick feeling inside my digestive tract. A financial cushion is not something I require of a romantic companion, and to force-feed this belief down my spiritual throat would be nothing short of toxic.

One of your greatest strengths in the pursuit of healthy intimate relationships is recognizing these ARODs and steering clear of anything that does not prove nourishing for you.

Journal Time

Take a moment to consider the ARODs you have heard.
What unhealthy behaviors have you consciously or
unconsciously adopted, and how have they affected
your relationships?

_____

_____

_____

_____

_____

_____

_____

_____

_____

_____

_____

_____

_____

The Danger of Empty Calories

*The definition of hell is two people in a relationship that
is starved for love and unable to fulfill that need.*
–Shannon L. Alder

A dear friend of mine, Amanda, is pretty. She is the kind of blonde-haired, blue-eyed beauty that, despite the forty-six years inscribed on her driver's license, can model for one of those Abercrombie & Fitch boards fit only for the god-like athletes. Not only that, she does the right thing when no one is looking, can make drool-worthy brisket, and can make you laugh until you're wishing you had worn Depends.

Unfortunately, Amanda's spouse of eighteen years cheated on her for ten of those years. Apparently, he didn't see the amazing woman he married, as he was too occupied "falling in love" with his secretary.

Maybe their relationship was doomed from the start; maybe they just weren't compatible and it took sharing space and three kids together to discover said incompatibility.

Regardless, Amanda tried to hold on to her husband and their marriage. She repeatedly said, "We were so good on paper."

But paper isn't life. You can be the same religion and share similar bank accounts, spending habits, and parenting styles—even share allergies (pollen, apparently)—and yet be horribly ill-suited for each other in the day-to-day *je ne sais quoi* ephemeral-yet-real arena.

My friend even *knew* they didn't meet the *je ne sais quoi* criteria for long-term companionship. For years, whenever Amanda spoke about her now ex, it would be with a figurative and sometimes even a literal sigh. That sigh is the nutritional equivalent of standing in front of an open fridge, expecting something different to appear. But the inside of our fridge doesn't change just because we want it to. Everything in there is just as it was when you popped your head in twenty minutes earlier.

Each time Amanda fought to "keep" her husband, each time she pushed aside her own figurative sighs, she was opening up a fridge full of empty calories that rendered her unsatisfied. And her spouse was more than content to do the same until he got caught with another "dish."

Once the affair was out, Amanda's husband was eager to articulate what they both knew deep down: their union was way past its expiration date. No doubt he was a major coward, not coming clean about his activity in someone else's "fridge" (Amanda found out all on her own). But once the caloric misfortune was addressed, he was eager for each of them to physically and emotionally move on.

Not Amanda. She wanted to keep looking inside their marital fridge, desperate to find some crumb to provide them with sustenance. It didn't matter that she was starving for gluten-free products and he was hankering for beef stew; she refused to let either one of them out of the house to search for other foods. Gosh darn it, they were going to MAKE something work out of the stale and dying products in their one-and-only fridge.

Fortunately, it only takes one person to make a divorce happen. It forced my emotionally and physically malnourished friend to close the fridge she had shared with her husband of eighteen years.

After her divorce, Amanda was faced with a brand-new fridge. This one was pristine, devoid of memories, and free of ho-hum meals. An empty fridge, depending on your outlook, can be a rewarding opportunity, a culinary starting point full of gustatory possibilities!

Amanda was terrified of the new spacious fridge. In her eyes, it desperately *needed* filling. The mere idea of exploring farmers markets in search of healthy produce that would nourish her caused her heart to beat a bit too fast for her liking. Amanda didn't see her empty fridge as a wonderful opportunity to discover things she had secretly wanted for years. She felt extremely uneasy leaving it empty for even a second. It didn't matter what kind or quality of food was in her new place, so long as it was filled with something, almost anything really.

Within a month of her divorce, Amanda started dating. Her goal? *To find someone.* Our intentions are powerful. Amanda's intention of finding "someone" filled her fridge with much different produce than the intention of healing and taking time to nourish herself.

It's almost a year since Amanda's divorce, almost a year since she began an intimate relationship with "someone."

"He's so kind. And he's patient with me. I keep telling him that I don't love him, but he says he's okay with that. I don't know why I feel this way. He's so good to me. I feel like something's missing. When I tell him this, he says it's okay. I feel so bad about it. But he's really such a good guy. It's hard to find good guys."

Amanda repeats these words almost every time we meet. And I can hear the mournful sigh in her voice, not altogether different from the figurative sigh she expressed a year ago regarding her marriage. Why?

Amanda may have swapped "fridges," but the calories remain the same: empty. Until she takes the brave steps to mourn and reflect on her failed marriage, she is likely to repeat a pattern of settling, of holding on to intimate relationships that don't nourish.

Many of us eat when we aren't hungry, eager for that hit of dopamine to dampen or suspend our emotional pain or frustration. When we do this in our relationships, we are paying a hefty price in emotional, spiritual, and physical well-being. I believe we are actually stalling our growth when we choose intimate relationships that we know don't "feed" us.

There's nothing wrong with empty calories when we accept them for what they are (the one-night stand, for example). The danger is staying in a relationship where one or both of you want more than the other can give. Amanda is clearly not in love with her new (albeit loyal) love; he is a nutritional security blanket that is inadvertently delaying the healing process of her neglected broken heart. She is also preventing her new beau from exploring a relationship with someone out there who might just consider him the best thing since sliced bread. As long as these two continue to do the caloric tango of empty calories, neither will grow. Amanda's swapped one stagnant diet for another.

Journal Time

We all have empty calories in our lives in the form of people who temporarily "fill us up" but often render us lonelier than we were before engaging in the relationship. Take a moment to consider any past or current partnerships you knew/know deep down weren't nourishing for you.

My empty-calorie relationship(s):

_____

_____

_____

_____

_____

_____

_____

_____

_____

_____

_____

What do I get out of my empty-calorie relationship(s)?

_____

_____

_____

_____

_____

_____

_____

_____

_____

_____

_____

_____

_____

What is the cost of staying in the relationship(s)?

_____

_____

_____

_____

_____

_____

_____

_____

_____

_____

_____

_____

_____

_____

The Best Dish

I've never fooled anyone. I've let people fool themselves.
They didn't bother to find out who and what I was. Instead
they would invent a character for me. I wouldn't argue with
them. They were obviously loving somebody I wasn't.
    −Marilyn Monroe

W hen my fridge was finally, blessedly empty, I found
myself all alone. After spending over fifteen years
with the same human being and sharing everything from
children to mortgages, I was staring at a cavernous "fridge"
yearning to be filled.

We've all had breakups, heartaches, and romantic
fissures that evoke a range of emotions—from holy-
crap-what-just-happened to what-is-the-point-of-ever-
emerging-from-bed. Most of us don't want to be alone;
most of us ache for a companion who can snuggle us and
make us laugh; someone who has our back, someone who
gets us.

So what do we typically do? We REPEAT, filling our
fridge with products that might sound different and offer
a slightly different flavor but are, deep down, the same dish
we've been consuming for years.

A friend of mine, Anjie, came over to tell me that she
and her husband were splitting. With tears of rage in her
eyes, she confided, "He grabbed my daughter by the neck
and threw her to the ground."

Anjie has three kids, one of whom requires constant
medical attention. Her ten-year-old daughter is the one
who is currently sporting her stepfather's hand marks on

the back of her neck and throat. Anjie is terrified at the thought of leaving her husband, yet she knows it's what NEEDS to happen.

Anjie is the breadwinner. Anjie is the one who takes care of all three kids (including the five-year-old, who requires intense medical care and is now faced with losing her dad). She has blue eyes the color of a spring sky and sun-kissed hair. She wears her heart on her sleeve and still manages to run her business assertively.

And yet, Anjie is terrified. "I thought I knew him. We were friends for six years before we started dating. This is my second relationship where the man treats me—and now my daughter—like shit."

I gently corrected her. "No. This is your third. Let's not forget your father. He taught you it was okay to be mistreated."

We learn these cycles of filling ourselves up with the same crap from our guardians, our first role models, the ones we trust without question (at least in our formative years), the ones we consider "normal," the ones whose ARODs are either purposely or subconsciously ingrained in our psyche.

Anjie is afraid to date ever again. "I don't trust myself. I'm afraid of repeating the same pattern."

My dear friend first needs to clean out her fridge. But even then it's not time to start looking for new produce. It's time to get to know the best dish ever: herself.

We all have patterns. The key is to recognize our patterns and name our psychological Achilles' heel. This happens when we are willing to go bravely into the wilderness of ourselves, the place we hide from the world. It is a place that requires us to get still and listen. We typically don't like to enter a quiet space. It is, after all, asking for the cobwebs and unpleasant terrain of our past to emerge.

Here's the tough cookie we all need to swallow if we want to experience healthy relationships: if we don't go inside, those cobwebs and nasty bits are only going to grow stronger and more insistent.

Dear reader, there's no easy way around this, no swiping right or left to move forward, no quick weight loss solution to a new and improved you. And yes, there are those scary cliffs from our younger years we might not want to face, but there's also beauty found in the landscape of our past.

Look at Anjie. She is a tower of strength who still takes her father's abuse to heart. Until she stands up to his abuse, she will continue to think little of herself no matter how much her actions and life prove what a powerful woman she is.

When my ex has our children, I often go on dates with myself: I treat myself to a mani-pedi or take a juicy book to my favorite restaurant. I go for long walks, practice yoga, meditate. I carve out time to write in a journal or sit outside with a mug of coffee, just taking in the trees.

I spent my twenties and thirties ignoring or pushing aside my voice. If I'm honest with myself, I don't even know if I *knew* my voice or how to find it. I was too busy trying to please everyone, too occupied altering my core Self in order to please my spouses and ignore the fact I was walking on eggshells.

So after my divorce, I decided to hit the pause button on my pattern of serial monogamy, filling my fridge with variations of the same crap. I decided that nothing was going in my fridge until I knew myself, until I could understand my nutritional affinity for attracting controlling men, until I could figure out why I often lost my identity in intimate relationships.

Going for a manicure might seem like a small act, but in the world of personal growth, it is an opportunity for internal transformation. So is reading a book alone in a restaurant or going for a walk solo. The activity doesn't matter; it's the message we are sending to our psyche that matters. Over time that message packs one hell of a nutritional punch: you matter.

When we remember that we matter, we want to slow down and pay attention. We want to take the time to discover the tapestry of our past and present. We want to revel in the journey of self-discovery and embrace each moment.

So I delve into the act of journaling and walking solo when I'm divining my inner voice. Others may thrive when they're dirt biking an open road or sleeping under a blanket of stars. The road we take doesn't matter, so long as we are willing to engage in self-reflection along the way.

Here's the delicious truth: YOU are the best dish. Regardless of what messages your parents purposely or inadvertently transmitted to you, you can keep what works and discard the rest, replacing it with messages that resonate with you, those that light your spiritual path.

Anjie knows she won't find what she's looking for in other men; she knows she needs to break the pattern (or as she calls it, "the curse") before she can consider another intimate relationship. Though she'll be busy cleaning out her fridge, her willingness to do so puts her on the path to self-discovery.

Before we start looking to fill our fridge, let's create some time to discover ourselves: the Best Dish.

Journal Time

What messages did your parent(s) impart to you growing up?

_____

_____

_____

_____

_____

_____

_____

_____

_____

_____

_____

_____

_____

_____

_____

How have early messages from your caregivers affected you as an adult?

_____

_____

_____

_____

_____

_____

_____

_____

_____

_____

_____

_____

_____

What's your relationship pattern(s)? Why do you think that is?

_____

_____

_____

_____

_____

_____

_____

_____

_____

_____

_____

_____

_____

_____

_____

What activities help you hear your inner voice?

_____

_____

_____

_____

_____

_____

_____

_____

_____

_____

_____

_____

_____

_____

Rebound Cake

No relationship is a waste of time. The wrong ones teach
you the lessons that prepare you for the right ones.
—Anonymous

How could you be with someone who isn't over their ex?
That makes you a rebound. Are you a side order?
Are you a garlic bread?
—Anonymous

Until you get comfortable with being alone, you'll never
know if you're choosing someone out of love or loneliness.
—Mandy Hale

When my fridge was empty, I was still in mourning. The clean shelves and spacious compartments did not exempt me from being bombarded by the questions that regularly flooded my brain: *Could I have tried harder to make it work? Was he really "that" controlling? Will I make it on my own?*

The ending of a relationship is a bit like death: We are left with memories that involve all of our senses; we replay the good parts and relentlessly second-guess certain moments. We are still affected by the sound of our ex's voice, sometimes taunted by a song on the radio that reminds us of them. Such moments stir bittersweet memories and make it that much more painful to navigate the territory of our broken hearts.

As we would with a death, we go through the stages in our own idiosyncratic fashion and at our own pace: denial, anger, bargaining, depression, and acceptance. One minute we are looking with teary eyes at photos from "the good old days" and the next we are ripping these same coveted pictures with zest and recycling them in the nearest bin (most likely the kitchen since we are already cleaning out that fridge).

After years of walking on eggshells, years of living in a controlled environment (my ex kept cameras inside and outside of our home; there were certain foods he didn't want me to eat; he made it clear I was not to work outside the home), hindsight shows me now that it was no accident I was doubting my decision to leave. For over fifteen years, my voice didn't matter; for almost two decades, I knew all about deferring to someone else's opinion on a matter but next to nothing about listening to (or finding!) my own thoughts. So when I finally left, it didn't matter how many dear friends told me how proud they were of my strength for finding the courage to leave; *I* needed to discover and feel what was often told to me; *I* needed to mourn the person I had allowed myself to recede into over those fifteen years.

There's a well-known experiment involving fleas in a glass jar. When they are first put into a jar, they'll immediately jump out. But when they are placed in that jar with a glass lid over the top, the fleas will start hitting against that glass lid and eventually fall back down to the bottom of the jar. After a while, the fleas grow conditioned to the presence of that glass lid, still jumping (as fleas do) but purposely below the glass lid (even fleas, apparently, want to protect themselves).

Here's where the powerful conditioning manifests: when we remove the glass "ceiling" of that jar, the fleas *remain in the jar*, never once questioning their ability to jump past the height of the lid *that's no longer there!*

After leaving my partner, I was like one of those fleas. Despite the fact that I was adjusting to living alone, I was so conditioned to not question or think for myself, so trained to limit myself and walk on those eggshells, that I was, as a dear friend of mine says, "low-hanging fruit."

There is nothing more vulnerable than someone who doesn't know who she or he is. There is also nothing more dangerous.

I'm a believer in the Universe giving us exactly what we need to grow, whether we recognize it or not. I also believe we attract what we need and who we are, so in hindsight, it's no surprise that I crossed paths with Neil: one of my greatest lessons.

According to *Merriam-Webster*,[7] two of the many definitions for *rebound* are contradictory: the action of recoiling *and yet* upward leap or movement. A rebound relationship is a bit of a contradictory notion as well. True, we are moving on, into the territory of a new relationship; however, we are simultaneously recoiling or drawing back as a consequence of our previous relationship(s).

Rebound relationships can be delicious, and my rebound cake with Neil was no exception. Being with Neil was *nothing like* (there's that recoiling element—the act of moving back, in the opposite direction of a past relationship) the caloric famine I had experienced with my former

---

7   *Merriam-Webster, s.v.* "rebound," accessed October 2, 2019, https://www.merriam-webster.com/dictionary/rebound.

partner. Consciously, I didn't want anyone at all like my ex, so I subconsciously rebounded (upward, opposing momentum) into a nutrient-rich relationship where many of my needs were finally met.

Neil did not want to control me (one of the pithy sayings he coined is literally "I never want to control, change, or fix anyone"). He honored my voice and embraced my creative spirit. He made me laugh. In the attraction department, we both had goo-goo eyes for each other, articulating the other's beauty both inside and out. We became the other's champion and best friend.

Alas, the Universe gives us what we need, not necessarily what we want. I met Neil when I was still raw, unsure of myself, and still divining my voice. Yes, he was the polar opposite of my ex, but he was also a little too much like me: both of us had experienced abusive relationships with our former partners, both of us were starving for affection, both of us were people pleasers who had a tendency to put ourselves last.

I am so grateful for my flavorful rebound cake with Neil. He showed me that the kind, sensitive, funny, and intelligent soul I longed for existed. He taught me to appreciate facets of myself I took for granted or had never even considered special. He demonstrated what it looks and feels like to have someone respect my opinion.

So why the rebound cake? Why not the never-ending Viennese table of love between us? Again, I believe we attract what we are and what we want, and when I met Neil, I was a commitment-phobe, and so was he. During the time we dated, he helped me discover that it was safe to leap out of my figurative flea jar, valuing my opinions and acknowledging—no *commending*—my accomplishments, big and small. I demonstrated that it was okay to state my opinion, articulate my needs, and express vulnerability without receiving a verbal attack. We were, as Neil likes to say, "twins." We were each other's reflections.

My rebound cake relationship was a therapeutic one. We each taught the other it was possible to love and be loved unconditionally—ours was an I-have-your-back kind of love. The outer frosting of romance was delicious and fun, but it was the rich chocolate cake (only good can come from chocolate) between us that will always remain: our friendship.

For all of our twin-like qualities, Neil and I did not see eye-to-eye on the long-distance nature of our relationship. It was enough for me, but not for Neil. Once I accepted this (I'm sharing the CliffNotes version here—you know we had heartache and a couple of heavy fridge-cleaning sessions too), I could return to the foundation of friendship on which our relationship had started.

We still talk and laugh (boy, do we laugh). I could say that it's purely distance that keeps us from getting back together romantically, but deep down, I don't think that's the real reason. Our alikeness, the very thing that brings us close together, is what can also foster an unhealthy (intimate) relationship over time: our sensitive natures, our affinity for worrying, our need to please—these qualities can cause unintentional emotional turmoil.

Journal Time

Neil was my chocolate cake rebound. Our frosting was the sweet romance, but the dense chocolate cake inside is the friendship that endures. I will always be grateful to Neil for teaching me to love every facet of myself and for helping me psychologically flee my flea jar (pun intended!).

Choose a rebound relationship that stands out for you. What kind of dessert or food item would you compare it to and why?

_____

_____

_____

_____

_____

_____

_____

_____

_____

Where were you emotionally/mentally/physically when you met your rebound?

_____

_____

_____

_____

_____

_____

_____

_____

_____

_____

_____

_____

_____

_____

What kind of "calories" did you receive from your rebound (e.g., helpful, harmful, insightful)?

_____

_____

_____

_____

_____

_____

_____

_____

_____

_____

_____

_____

_____

How did you change after your rebound relationship?

_____

_____

_____

_____

_____

_____

_____

_____

_____

_____

_____

_____

_____

_____

Why the Coffee Date?

This morning, with her, having coffee.
—Johnny Cash, when asked for his description of paradise

Coffee is the universal beverage of the dating world. The caffeinated drink offers a conduit to potential intimate relationships. It is synonymous with first impressions and is the beverage of choice for commitment-phobes and intimacy-seekers alike. Over a cup of coffee is where you discover your soul mate or determine you are sharing a drink with the next serial killer.

When I first ended my relationship with my partner of more than fifteen years, I naively assumed the dating world was not much different from the one I had known in the nineties: you like someone, the attraction is mutual, you go out for dinner. Wrong! In the twenty-first-century pace of life, once food is involved, the stakes are silently but palpably higher.

I learned this lesson firsthand when a man asked me out. It was dinnertime and I was hungry, so I suggested we meet at a nearby Mexican restaurant.

"Wow! I'm impressed! You just jump right in and agree to have a meal with me. You don't waste any time, do you?" he asked.

Unfortunately, my first date (Bryon) made this announcement once I was already sitting at dinner with him and realizing I had committed to spending at least an hour with a stranger I could already tell I didn't want to spend another minute with. Only now, I was about to share a meal with this insensitive, aggressive, and sexually perverse stranger (more about Bryon in the chapter "The Buffet Line Myth").

By suggesting dinner, I had apparently signaled to Bryon that I was very much into him. As a commitment-phobe, I felt like Penelope the cat, smothered by that love-obsessed stalking skunk, Pepé Le Pew. Every other word out of his mouth was of a sexual nature. I had recurring visions of the ceiling opening up and ejecting Pepé Le Pew into a galaxy far from ours.

Coffee dates—they're the only way to go. Drinks are much easier to share with a stranger than a meal. If the conversation goes well, the date can always "graduate" to time together with actual food.

Coffee is the great litmus test of chemistry, the easier, bottom-line barometer of potentiality, the ubiquitous equalizer (after all, a brain surgeon and a hairdresser can both afford a cup of java). A coffee date doesn't come with frosting and fondant, there's no fondue or flambé to distract you from determining if there's going to be a second date.

Coffee is direct and without pretense. The coffee date is not a euphemism for casual sex. Worldwide, when people partake in a coffee date, their expectations operate at the most basic level: Will we connect? Will there be chemistry? Will I find this person attractive? Will I want to see this person again? How do I feel around this person?

We've emptied our fridges, people! We are not going to fill them with caloric mistakes. We are simply sharing a stimulating beverage with someone who might or might not be stimulating to us (and vice versa). The risks are low, but the potential is limitless.

The coffee date offers an authentic opportunity for human connection. The *idea* of the coffee date itself offers an opportunity for self-reflection. Recently, I was asked on a date with someone. I agreed to meet, but my heart wasn't on board with it. Just being asked created this inner reaction of resistance.

The Universe is made up of energy; WE are made of energy. So again, it should be no surprise that my potential coffee date and I could not seem to align our schedules to meet. And when an umpteenth tentative plan looked like it was going to actually happen, I received the man's text:

> *In the interest of full disclosure, I wanted to share with you that I am not sure what's going on with me. It has been a year and half since my divorce, and I thought I was ready to move on with my life and begin to date. But every time I get close, something seems to take over and compel me not to want to go. I honestly am just not ready apparently.*

Receiving this text was no accident. We were both carrying similar feelings about relationships and dating, but Michael was bold and mature enough to articulate it. In that moment, he became a new friend. We remain in the land of texting, and I am more than okay with this.

Michael recently texted, disclosing that he still wakes up "thinking some huge mistake occurred while I was sleeping and I'm accidentally living someone else's life today." Like all of us, he needs to examine the contents of his fridge and do a thorough cleaning.

Authenticity is one of our greatest powers; each of us is unique, so our decision to be our unfiltered selves (yes, even if we are a work in progress—perhaps even more so *because* we are a magnificent, messy work in progress) is a gift to ourselves, and ALL of our relationships. What a gift my new texting friend Michael is: demonstrating his self-awareness, articulating his concerns and confusion, heeding his inner voice even when he doesn't understand it.

Wow. The power of a coffee date, even one that doesn't physically manifest but sits in the mind as an idea between two people. That's some solid nutrition!

Journal Time

When we embark on a coffee date, we are choosing to partake in a meeting of the mind and heart with another person. Apart from the beverage in your hands, there is nothing but dialogue (or lack thereof) for entertainment. Imagine your "perfect" coffee date, the kind of meeting that finds you eager to share a meal with this person.

What does your conversation with your perfect coffee date involve?

_____

_____

_____

_____

_____

_____

_____

_____

_____

_____

_____

What can your coffee date say or do that will be an
immediate turnoff or red flag for you?

_____

_____

_____

_____

_____

_____

_____

_____

_____

_____

_____

_____

_____

_____

Know Your Comfort Food

Ice cream was reliable. Young men were not.
−Kerry Greenwood, *Murder in the Dark*

Charity couldn't bring herself to cry on Lady Beddington's shoulder−not until after she'd mopped up a plate or two of spaghetti with buckets of cheap red wine.
−Elizabeth Jane Howard, *Mr. Wrong*

During my divorce, my lawyer hit on me.

"You deserve pleasure. It gets lonely at night. I want you to know you can call me any hour of the night." He took my fingers in his well-manicured hands. "I'm here to give you pleasure. It can get lonely at night; you'll see. It can get very lonely, and I just want you to know that I'm here for you. Just call me."

I fired him.

Creepy passes and disbarring behavior aside, the sixty-two-year-old litigator was primitively and unprofessionally articulating his ego's need for his preferred comfort food. He was, in psychological terms, projecting.

I'm well aware that Mr. Pervert Pants (Mr. PP, a.k.a. my FORMER litigator) was referring to sex, but the way he soliloquized about loneliness told me, in hindsight (at the time, I felt like a deer in the headlights), that he was speaking from experience, projecting his hunger for connection and affection onto his client. He eagerly offered to make me a chocolate soufflé, insisting he made "the best" soufflé and that I would "have to come over" to his house to taste it.

Again, while Mr. PP was genuinely referring to an edible dessert, it's obvious that was the caloric conduit to lure me into his bed.

Mr. PP had been married four times; he is one of those men who walks through life sans a filter, sharing a bit too much, trying a bit too hard to "fit in" with the other lawyers. He's impulsive, displaying a false bravado that can be torn asunder with one questioning look.

While I felt violated and betrayed by Mr. PP, I also knew he wore his heart on his sleeve and didn't have any malicious intent toward me. Yes, he advised me terribly (a family lawyer who lives with vulnerability is both an oxymoron and a recipe for one weak divorce litigator); yes, he was inappropriate; but Mr. PP naively thought there was dating potential between us.

Hell to the no.

Basically, Mr. PP thought with his penis.

Or did he? Was he starving for comfort, the comfort he hoped would put a moratorium on his loneliness—a loneliness that had caused him to cross boundaries and risk his very career? Was that craving for affection and connection preventing him from thinking rationally?

There are people who are married and starving for affection. I was one of them. I'm alone now but not at all lonely. You can be with someone and feel more alone than if you were in solitude. It's all about keeping the right company, and I prefer my own company to the ill-suited kind.

But for many, comfort food isn't edible at all. Comfort food offers us a temporary reprieve from our struggles and suffering. We hunger for a connection, a longing to be understood and to understand; we might even thirst for something we can't articulate but know is missing or lacking in our lives.

Besides the more familiar caloric ones, below are some common yet overlooked comfort "foods" we use to temporarily fill us:

- one-night stands
- watching movies/TV
- gambling
- reading
- playing an instrument
- porn
- alcohol/marijuana
- texting/tweeting
- sleeping pills
- shopping

None of the above items are "bad" or "wrong," just as none of the edible comfort foods we ingest are negative. We all have bad days and, since you're reading this book, I'm guessing you've experienced your fair share of rocky intimate relationships. And thank goodness for the pleasure, the sheer reprieve from stress or unhappiness that comfort food provides. But there are two caveats to enjoying comfort food:

1. Comfort food, like everything else, runs on a continuum. If you are buying a new dress to cheer yourself up after a breakup, that's one thing, but if your comfort food involves maxing out your credit cards and subsequently filing for bankruptcy, your

comfort food is no good for you. It is a red flag that something needs to be addressed on the inside.

2. KNOW your comfort food(s) and the WHY behind your hankerings. If Mr. PP had waxed a tad introspective, he may have thought twice about making a pass at his client.

The spectrum of comfort food runs from an innocuous moment of pleasure all the way to the world of addiction. Comfort food can also postpone growth, deferring our chances of experiencing authentic friendship and intimacy.

The comfort food is only the symptom, the manifestation of a need or needs not being met. The media has popularized the story of the obese man or woman who has gastric bypass surgery, quickly losing hundreds of pounds, only to discover that he or she continues to struggle with issues of low self-esteem. Whatever form our comfort food takes, the key is recognizing the desire *behind* the action.

Author Julia Cameron writes candidly about her comfort food of choice: alcohol.[8]

In 1978, in January, I stopped drinking…. For me, the trick was always getting past the fear and onto the page. I was playing beat the clock—trying to write before the booze closed in like fog and my window of creativity was blocked again…. I told myself that if sobriety meant no creativity I did not want to be sober. Yet I recognized that drinking would kill me *and* the creativity.

---

8   Julia Cameron, *The Artist's Way: A Spiritual Path to Higher Creativity* (New York: Jeremy P. Tarcher/Putnam, 2002), xiv.

In order to build an authentic friendship and a potential intimate relationship, we first need to get real with ourselves. Just as the incredibly talented Julia Cameron discovered she could soar in her creative writing endeavors[9] sans alcohol, we need to let go of any dangerous or potentially hindering comfort food before entering into a romantic relationship.

Mr. PP's four marriages are the fallout from not recognizing his comfort food, from not taking the necessary time for reflection.

When I was with my former husband, my comfort food involved downing chips and ice cream each night in front of my beloved boob tube. Despite my desire for intimacy, sex was a rare event in our codependent relationship. Affection, in any form, was offered in crumbs spiced with derision. Our dialogue frequently went like this:

Me: Don't you want to?

Him: I'm tired.

Me: We could just kiss.

Him: That's just a tease.

Me: We could hold each other.

Him: Life is not a Nicholas Sparks movie. We are not in *The Notebook*.

Frustrated and unhappy, I needed pleasure, and so I found it in junk food. While I'm grateful for my fast metabolism, delving into gustatory satisfaction provided nothing more than a quick hit of dopamine to delay the inevitable truth silently screaming in my soul: my marriage was failing.

---

9   Julia Cameron is, among other things, an award-winning journalist and screenwriter for Hollywood films and television.

If we listen, our comfort foods speak volumes about where we are in our relationships and how we feel about ourselves. Our bodies are our temples, and here I was filling my temple with junk food instead of dealing with the reality of a man who wouldn't or couldn't connect. I literally and figuratively did not feel filled, so I found perfunctory satisfaction in high levels of carbohydrates and processed sugars.

It's worth noting that now that I'm divorced, I don't crave an unending bowl of popcorn or a tub of Dreyer's. Don't get me wrong—I still love these things, but I'm satisfied after a normal serving size.

Journal Time

Our comfort foods offer a litmus test for our overall satisfaction in relationships. Take a moment to consider your comfort foods. What do you receive from these foods (e.g., satisfaction, pleasure, wholeness, accomplishment, release, etc.)?

_____

_____

_____

_____

_____

_____

_____

_____

_____

_____

_____

How long do the positive effects of your comfort food last? How do you feel when they wear off or stop working?

_____

_____

_____

_____

_____

_____

_____

_____

_____

_____

_____

_____

_____

_____

What would your life be like without this comfort food? How might you feel about yourself after bidding your comfort food farewell?

_____

_____

_____

_____

_____

_____

_____

_____

_____

_____

_____

_____

_____

The Buffet Line Myth

*I lurched away from the table after a few hours feeling like
Elvis in Vegas—fat, drugged, and completely out of it.*
—Anthony Bourdain

When virtual reality gets cheaper than dating, society is doomed.
—Scott Adams, *Dogbert*

Online dating in the twenty-first century is a veritable buffet line: there may be a few great dishes out there, but for the most part, there aren't a whole lot of meals you want to dig into.

A close friend of over twenty years called me recently. She asked me how the dating scene was going. *Er…how's it going? Let's see…*

> There's Bryon, who told me, "I'm not a drinker, but once a year I like to get trashed and then have sex for twenty-four hours straight."
>
> There's Steve, who left me a passive-aggressive text when I thanked him for our date but said I didn't think we would be a good fit.
>
> There's Alex, who asked me, "Everyone always wants to know what it's like to have sex with the same gender, right?"
>
> There's Dylan, who explained that the girlfriend he "loved" had gotten into a bad accident. She's now "a mess," so "of course we broke up."

How I wish these were fictionalized anecdotes! Unfortunately, their names are the only fictional element. The stories themselves are painfully true.

My friend, upon hearing my dating tales, laughed and said, "I was helping my friend find a man on Match this week. After looking with her, I was so grateful I'm a lesbian."

Whatever your sexual orientation, navigating the dating world is challenging. I continue to consider the buffet line of online potential suitors. My buddy Neil (my fellow twin) is doing the same, and here are some of the common threads we've noticed:

- Very few people actually read another person's profile.
- Men love to pose standing near or sitting inside an expensive car or holding a fish.
- Women either sport a Botox face (no smile) or don't offer a full-body shot.
- Both men and women offer pictures with sunglasses or photos taken from so far away they could be either gender.
- Women either hide behind clothing so you can't really see their form or seem to enjoy posting suggestive poses. (Neil says a popular one is doing a handstand split on the beach…Seriously?)

Since writing this book, I've made a handful of male friends. It's insightful to hear their turnoffs and to discover that they are pretty consistent, regardless of age or lifestyle.

Here are the top online/buffet line turnoffs for men I've discovered:

- Lying about your age
- Writing in your profile: must make $150K+
- Not offering a clear full-body picture
- Posting pictures from over a decade ago

- Posting TMI in your profile (e.g., My ex was never there for my kids, so the next man I'm going to be with needs to know that my kids come first)

My friend Lorie (my best bud of over two decades) and I talked about the biggest turnoffs for women found in the buffet line of online dating. Here's what we came up with:

- Lying about your age
- Not bothering to read my profile but writing me anyway
- Posting pictures from over a decade ago
- Posting bare-chested pictures of yourself
- Posting selfies surrounded by big-lipped and big-breasted babes

Neil was the only male buddy who felt it was a turnoff to only write based on pictures, without taking the time to actually read the person's profile. It's fascinating to me that both genders are frustrated or turned off by similar behaviors.

To my female readers, I'd like to say that nothing good can ever come from putting a price on a man's company—or anyone's company, for that matter. Sure, if you are only looking for someone to take care of you fiscally, I suppose that could work. But what about making ambition, honesty, integrity, and compassion your criteria for a partner? What about writing a profile that comes from your core values? What about writing a profile that speaks about kindness and tenacity? I was in a marriage where money was not an issue, where I could buy whatever my heart desired. Yet there was a price I paid for that lifestyle: control. Yes, we need money to live, but to make money a CRITERIA for compatibility is a recipe for heartache.

I'd like to tell my male readers that you do not need a fancy car or an impressive fish in your hands to woo a genuine person. The right person is someone who doesn't need those material accoutrements to be happy; the right person will be with you because of YOU, your essence, your awesome company. And when you feel compelled to hold an expensive cigar or scantily clad women on your arms, you are screaming insecurity; you are telling the buffet line of the online dating world that you are not enough on your own.

I have nothing against buffets. They're actually kind of fun, an edible adventure to discover which dishes will be a hit and which will be a definite miss. But from my experience, it seems that the overall quality of dining out goes down when there are too many different kinds of dishes to prepare. The same is true in the endless world of online dating. Between Tinder, Match, OkCupid (the list goes on…and on…), you can get a cramp in your hand just from swiping through so many profiles!

Online dating in the twenty-first century is truly a paradox: we have all of this boundless potential, yet it's easy to feel more isolated and alone than ever before in human history. We even have a new vocabulary to help navigate this unchartered cyberspace territory:

- *ghosting* (which has nothing to do with actual ghosts) is abandoning a new romantic partner sans explanation.

- *catfishing* is pretending to be someone else (e.g., posting a fake picture on your profile).
- *winking*, *poking*, *liking*, and *favoriting* (who knew *favorite* could morph into a verb?) are all ways in which you can communicate your interest online without ever typing a word or leaving the comfort of your home.

And maybe that's the problem. Our ability to go through the buffet line, the *hundreds* of buffet lines, desensitizes, disenchants, and disheartens us. We look without really seeing, judge without really knowing, expect without really trying. The art of authentic communication gets lost in a world where canned questions can be addressed to total strangers, where it becomes a little too easy to click on a mass-produced question instead of creating your own:

- *What is one of your favorite childhood memories?*
- *What's your favorite cocktail? Do you have a signature drink?*
- *Who has been the biggest influence in your life?*
- *If you were going to hang out with one of the Spice Girls, which one would you pick and why?*
- *What's your most embarrassing moment?*

There's nothing wrong with any of those questions, but you need to know a bit about a person before sending any of them. After all, what if the person had an awful childhood? And if you are asking a recovering alcoholic for his favorite cocktail, that's not likely to elicit a positive response.

In order for us to find the buffet line of online dating rewarding, we have to get real with ourselves AND pay attention to what's being advertised.

I recently "met" a man online who found me attractive. His profile was short and sweet: self-effacing guy who feels uncomfortable writing about himself. He was on the young side (for me), single, and he did not have children. His profile stated that he was looking for a long-term relationship and marriage.

My profile stated my age (six years his senior), status (divorced with two kids), and that I was looking for a friend.

This young man, Sam, wrote to say how "gorgeous" I was, asking me for my number. Here's how the rest of our online chat session went:

Me: I'm flattered, but we are not looking for the same things.

Him: You're everything I could want in another person.

Me: You don't even know me! You write that you want to have kids someday. I don't want to have more children. That's a deal-breaker right there.

Him: No, not a deal-breaker. It's not ideal, but it's not a deal-breaker. Can I please have your number?

Me: It's late. If you still feel you want my number tomorrow, I'll send it your way.

As flattering as this dialogue was, I knew it was not going to go anywhere. I did not come out of a fifteen-year relationship and clean out my figurative refrigerator in order to ignore my needs and wants. Also, in good conscience, I did not want to encourage a relationship with a man who clearly wanted to be a father someday.

Sam is a handsome man with an endearing, self-deprecating humor. (He wrote the next morning to insist he hadn't changed his mind. Yes, I gave him my number.) He is one of those dishes at a buffet line that makes your mouth water with curiosity. But then you get closer (i.e., our phone dialogue) and it has a weird smell.

When something smells fishy, it's time to put the dish down and head back to the buffet to consider other items.

Sam was a little too self-deprecating, a little too eager with the compliments, a little too hungry for a relationship with me, a total stranger. Had I not spent time cleaning out my fridge and getting real about who I was and what I wanted, I could have easily ignored the red flags and pursued a relationship with him.

Our instincts, our gut feelings, never abandon us. Sometimes, we lose track of them in the grand buffet before us. But we all have the ability to wax self-reflective, no matter how distracting the selection.

I wrote Sam to tell him that I didn't think we would be a good fit, wishing him only the best. His texts came fast and furious, wanting to know why. After all, he was willing to buy my son a condo and wanted to "skip dating so we could just get married." (At first, I found his texts funny, but their frequency and content delved into the Land of Creepy. My friend Neil says, "Once you enter the Land of Creepy, you can't undo Creepy.")

Sam: U met a better-looking guy?
Me: My kids are my first priority. If you looked at my profile, I wrote that I'm looking for a friend. I'm not ready for anything more at this point.

Let's just say Sam found it crazy that I was looking for a friend on a dating site. His annoyed reaction told me volumes:

1. Sam didn't read my profile or at least didn't read it carefully.
2. Sam's anger over something as small as a profile selection was a potential red flag.
3. Sam was indeed a fishy dish that I needed to bid adieu.

I am not suggesting that Sam is a psycho-killer or serial stalker. He strikes me as a lonely guy with self-esteem issues, someone who is eager to be in a committed relationship, even if it means ignoring his desire to be a father someday. He also strikes me as someone who tends to project what he *wants* onto someone he doesn't know. We all fall prey to this behavior at one point or another; it was just particularly obvious with Sam, whose overzealous interest in me was based only on photos he found online along with a brief essay he apparently never took the time to read.

Journal Time

When we approach a buffet line, it's important to be present, discerning the potential winning dishes from the red flags. We often do this without thinking twice: noticing how quickly the beef and broccoli dish is refilled versus the untouched banana cream pie that's sitting under the heat lights and swarming with flies.

Yet discerning potential relationship material in the never-ending online dating buffet becomes much harder. We can't assume someone's profile is an accurate depiction of who s/he is. We can be swayed by someone's looks, ignoring the red flags of incompatibility from the start (e.g., He is Catholic and you are Muslim. She is a left-wing liberal and you are a Tea Party Republican).

To avoid getting "food poisoning" in the digital buffet line, take a moment to list your red flags, your deal-breakers. These will be different for everyone, so it's important to get quiet and take time to acknowledge the items on your list. To dodge caloric tragedy, refer back to this list whenever you are tempted by what looks like a succulent dish.

My buffet line online dating red flags/deal-breakers:

_____

_____

_____

_____

_____

_____

_____

_____

_____

_____

_____

_____

_____

The Beauty of Brooklyn:
Avoiding Microwave Madness

*Eilis: You remember that after I had dinner at
your house, you told me that you loved me?
[Tony nods, somber and nervous]
Eilis: Well, I didn't really know what to say. But I
know what to say now. I have thought about you
and I like you, and I like seeing you, and maybe I feel
the same way. So the next time you tell me you love
me, if there is a next time, I'll say I love you too.*
—Brooklyn (2015)

*In this age of quick fixes and microwave mindsets, most of
us want what we want, and we want it right now...but just
as you can't force the farm to produce a harvest, you can't
force your seed of potential to grow until it is ripe and ready.*
—Derek Rydall

*My Saturday night is like a microwave burrito. Very tough
to ruin something that starts out so bad to begin with.*
—Michael Chabon

*You can't work three hours a week and make $100,000.
Get rich quick doesn't work. Crockpot mentality always
defeats microwave mentality.*
—Dave Ramsey

When Eilis (actress Saoirse Ronan) leaves Ireland
to pursue a better life in Brooklyn, New York, she
meets a young Italian man at a dance. They dance and talk.

The man, Tony (actor Emory Cohen), is smitten. He waits for Eilis to emerge every night from her bookkeeping class at Brooklyn College. They spend time talking at restaurants and at the beach. Tony brings her home to meet his family.

Tony and Eilis still have yet to engage in sexual activity. Yet they are best friends, clearly in love with each other, comfortable in their vulnerability. They know each other intimately before they have gotten physically intimate.

While Eilis and Tony are fictionalized characters of the 1950s from Nick Hornby's screenplay *Brooklyn*, there is a powerful recipe behind their intimate relationship that can be applied to our twenty-first-century dating world:

1. Take two people who are attracted to each other.
2. Give two people time together.
3. Give them more time together.
4. Add handfuls of vulnerability if steps 2 and 3 seem like a great dish.
5. Mix with honesty throughout.
6. Stir in time for self-reflection.
7. Allow time to simmer.
8. Prepare to enjoy your "dessert."

Everything in our society is fueled by impatience. We want "it," and we want whatever that elusive or specific thing is *now*. But relationships take time. We cannot swipe left or right or find an app on our smartphone that will enable a healthy, rewarding intimate relationship. We cannot Uber into the fast lane of compatibility with someone we have just met or create a filter through cyberspace that cuts out the painful parts of our journey of self-reflection.

I was twelve years old when my family got our first microwave. I remember feeling like Judy Jetson—the hip teenybopper in the futuristic cartoon series *The Jetsons*—who merely had to press a button and within minutes or even seconds, *voila!* Food was warm and ready to eat! No more waiting a half hour for last night's chicken dinner to be reheated in the toaster oven, no more standing over the stove, waiting for the oatmeal to thicken. Our family was ecstatic and reveled in the idea that our lives would be easier from then on and would relish oodles of free time to do other things.

But as I'm writing this well into the twenty-first century, we now know, of course, that while microwaves make our lives much easier, they are not a replacement for home cooking. Instant oatmeal in the microwave does not taste the same as homemade old-fashioned oats slow-cooked on the range. And if you've ever tried to make a cake in the microwave, you know that the flavor and texture don't compare to the same confection made in an oven.

Yet when we date, we seem to want the microwave version. We feel entitled to the speedy-search-for-romance style. What is our rush? The best meals I've ever tasted came from a crockpot or a sauté pan, which require a combination of ingredients to come together over a long time and cook or bake at the right temperature.

When we date, we need to give ourselves time to consider the other person and our reactions to that person. If we find ourselves instantly attracted, we *need* time for steps 4, 5, and 6 (vulnerability, honesty, and self-reflection), or else we are setting ourselves up for a potential burn. (Think overcooked popcorn in the microwave.)

Simmering (step 7) is just as important as the other dating steps because time together is when the real magic occurs. By the time my ex-husband and I had been dating for months, he was refusing to kiss me after I had eaten seafood because seafood isn't kosher. Therefore, until I brushed my teeth, I was unclean, he argued. This was the same man who wrote me poetry and opened car doors for me; the man who regularly said, "I want to take care of you," and took plane trips *every weekend but one* for a year to visit me.

But weekend visits are not the same as everyday time together. Had I allowed time for reflection, I would have acknowledged the stab of resentment I felt when my partner withheld that kiss because of my dietary choice. Had I allowed time for our relationship to simmer, I would have seen (assuming I was still self-reflecting) certain behaviors on his part that were hallmarks of a relationship recipe disaster.

As in cooking, when we "simmer" with someone, we affect each other. Sometimes the effect is nothing short of delicious, like onions and garlic browning in butter. But sometimes, we discover that two ingredients brought together can create a nasty combo, like eggplant and mushrooms. Both vegetables have the *potential* to be delicious together, but if you aren't aware that you need to salt the eggplant before sautéing, you'll end up with one bitter aubergine. And mushrooms, with their high moisture content, can end up tasteless if not permitted both time (low heat) and space (maximum surface on the pan) to caramelize.

I needed a slow flame with my former partner, time to consider the idea and potential reality of an "us." I needed time to see how we affected each other. And while I had reflected enough to tell him I didn't want to get married, my partner proposed to me anyway, merely five months after our meeting.

Oh, how I had wanted step 8! I wanted the sweet dessert of us, our "cheesy" (pun intended) Happily Ever After. I so wanted him to be who I needed him to be instead of addressing the concerns that were already plaguing my heart and mind. I needed to address that he hadn't yet shown me step 4 (vulnerability) and had fallen short from our first date on step 5 (honesty). I needed more time for step 6 (self-reflection) so I could acknowledge that I felt like I was losing my voice when I was with him (step 7), morphing from a strong woman into a dependent girl.

Unfortunately, I did what many of us do: I pushed aside my concerns and skipped ahead to the dessert (commitment), too hungry for connection to wait one second longer, settling for the microwave version of love instead of starting from scratch, and/or taking the time to find the right recipe and get it right!

I am not saying that the goal of an intimate relationship is perfection. Of course, we are all flawed human beings. Therefore, no relationship will ever be perfect. Perfection isn't the goal. The goal is healthy, rewarding relationships. Our cultural approach to romantic love doesn't seem to be working; it's why I set out to create a Friendship Diet in the first place. Step 8 isn't the end; it is the sweet reward and organic by-product that comes from *regularly doing* steps 2–7.

Eilis (from *Brooklyn*—a must-see flick that will render you itching to open your unicorn-covered journal), despite being a fictionalized character from the mid-twentieth century, is very much a modern woman. She doesn't allow herself to be "lost" to the charms of a man. She focuses on her education, agreeing to go out with Tony but never shirking her studies or job to spend time with him. She enjoys his company but waits several dates before she opens up a bit about her past—allowing for vulnerability but making certain he's "earned" that vulnerability. She maintains her loyalty with her family, heading back to Ireland to visit her sick mother for a month. She does not *need* Tony to go with her; it is understood she loves Tony but that visiting her sick mother is something she wants to handle independently.

Tony encourages her to meet his family after a handful of dates. He respects her decision to go home to Ireland solo. He respects the pace Eilis sets for their relationship.

The sex scene between Tony and Eilis is nothing short of explosive. And how could it not be when the couple has taken the time, real time, to know each other? (Yes, Hollywood does that whole montage-set-to-music "stuff," but it's understood that lots of time has passed.)

We deserve so much more than a Microwave Love (we've all seen that splattered-tomato-sauce look on the inside of the microwave when we've heated pasta a few seconds too long). Like Eilis and Tony, we deserve to meet someone who respects who we are, *exactly the way we are*. We deserve to be with someone who encourages vulnerability and authenticity in themselves and us. We deserve time for reflection, space to simmer with another person, *at a mutually respectful pace.* We deserve to be in a relationship that's built on honesty—with ourselves and our partner.

We also deserve to part ways and start all over again with someone new when one or most of those steps are not happening. The ingredients (people) might change, but the recipe (steps) remains the same.

Journal Time

Take a moment to reflect on either a current or past relationship. The more honest you are with yourself, the more potential for success with your intimate relationship—past, present, and future!

Step 1: Are/Were you attracted to this person?

_____

Step 2: Is/Was he/she attracted to you?

_____

Step 3: What is the nature of the time you spend together? (e.g., brief weekends, every day, etc.)

_____

_____

Step 4: How do you feel after spending more time with this person?

_____

_____

_____

Step 5: What is the vulnerability like for you and your partner?

_____

_____

_____

Step 6: Are there lies in your relationship? Are you lying? Do you suspect your partner is lying? If lies have come out, how has this affected your relationship?

_____

_____

_____

_____

Step 7: Take time for reflection. (Are your needs or your partner's needs being met? Are you or your partner addressing issues or ignoring them?)

_____

_____

_____

_____

Step 8: Simmer. (Do you or your partner affect each other positively or negatively, and how so?)

_____

_____

_____

_____

_____

_____

_____

_____

_____

_____

_____

_____

_____

_____

_____

A Well-Stocked Fridge Will
(Help) Keep Your Knickers On

*You have to participate relentlessly in the
manifestation of your own blessings.*
−Elizabeth Gilbert

We are human. We have needs. Ted knew this (*There's Something about Mary*) and went about "taking care of business" before heading out on a date with the girl of his dreams, Mary.

But it takes more than self-induced orgasms to keep poor decision-making at bay. When loneliness hits, consider these key caloric staples to prevent you from embarking on a relationship disaster or behaving regrettably:

1. Focus on work.
2. Make time for friends.
3. Plan things to look forward to.
4. Have an accountability buddy.
5. Keep a gratitude journal.
6. Meditate.
7. Pursue a hobby.
8. Exercise.

We can actively participate in all of the above good-for-us activities and still experience heavy cravings for company we know deep down is bad for us. We can get even more specific with the list above, adding things like swimming with dolphins in Barbados or parasailing in Tobago, and still hunger for a stranger's touch. We can exercise seven days a week in the toughest Krav Maga class around and still feel like giving in to our partner's wishes, even if it means ignoring our internal compass, to avoid being single again.

Loneliness can cause even the strongest heart to settle for less. There are many genuinely happy couples frolicking around while many unhappy couples masquerade happiness to both themselves and the world. One of my friends refers to his wife as "the boss" and is unable to make any decision without checking first with "the boss." Instead of addressing the bitter tone in his voice and the reason behind it, he continues to remain silent, staying at work as much as possible. With each kid they have (they're expecting number four—her desire, not his), the boss seems a little more omnipotent and my friend becomes a little less available at home.

My dear friend needs to restock his fridge with honesty and vulnerability. His voice needs to be heard and respected so that he can stop hiding in the office, afraid of the boss waiting for him at home. He deserves to be in a relationship where he can enjoy pulling off his knickers and know it doesn't mean making another baby.

Elizabeth Gilbert (author of *Big Magic: Creative Living Beyond Fear*) writes about author Mark Manson's philosophical question: "What's your favorite flavor of shit sandwich?" Gilbert explains that whatever we pursue in life (career, creativity, etc.) will involve some sort of sacrifice or…shit. The same is true for our intimate relationships. If we want to experience a rewarding connection in a mutually committed partnership, we need to accept that it's not always going to be rainbows and unicorns. There may be hours, days, and months where we ache for companionship, crave to be held, and feel starved for affection.

The shit sandwich of pursuing a rewarding and intimate relationship is swallowing the stings and arrows of rejection, heartache, and loneliness. It means dishing out bouts of painful willpower to say no to your friend with benefits; saying no to what your partner wants to hear and yes to what you need to say; saying no to one-night stands; saying no to someone you're intensely attracted to but know could not handle steps 4 through 8 (see the previous chapter in case you missed the recipe).

Neil has become my accountability buddy. His friendship is like a power-packed vitamin to keep me focused. The other day I told him I had met the cutest guy, who happened to be looking to share his life with someone who "lived a Christ-centered life" on a farm and loved camping.

Here's how Neil kept my knickers on:

Me: He's gorgeous.

Neil: You're not Christian.

Me: Is that *really* a deal-breaker?

Neil: You have never gone camping and you love living in the city.

Me: I could *learn* to love camping, and how hard could farm life be?

We both knew I was thinking with the wrong head. But Neil offered a reality check that wouldn't have happened had I kept my infatuation with Mr. Farmer to myself.

Would it have been the worst thing in the world to go on a date with Mr. Farmer? Probably not, but it wouldn't be fair to either one of us. After all, he deserves to find that Christ-centered partner just as much as I deserve to find companionship with someone who doesn't want a Christ-centered partner. At best, meeting would be the equivalent of sitting in front of a chocolate cake neither one of us can enjoy. At worst, it would mean taking a bite and wanting more, knowing it will cause either one or both of us to experience caloric heartbreak.

Journal Time

Take a moment to think with the right head. This is the person you are when you are already feeling satiated and not irrational with desire. The right head can also be thought of as your Highest Self and can be more easily found when we are well-rested and relaxed. The wrong head is that part of us that doesn't care about consequences. It typically emerges when we are hungry (physically, spiritually, or emotionally), exhausted, and feeling hopeless about a situation and, more importantly, ourselves.

Focusing on your Highest Self, consider where you are (either now or in the past) compromising, allowing your wrong head to make poor decisions for you.

Remember: Being in a committed relationship does not preclude us from thinking with the wrong head.

When I am thinking with the wrong head (e.g., fear-based, hunger-based, from a place of desperation and/or low self-esteem) I tend to:

_____

_____

_____

_____

_____

When I see my actions from my right head (a.k.a. my Highest Self), I see I'm doing these behaviors because I feel:

_____

_____

_____

_____

_____

I've decided to make _____ my accountability buddy. He/She will remind me to take responsibility for my actions and choices so that I can heed my right head and ignore my wrong head.

My list of key caloric staples I will turn to when loneliness hits:

1. _____

2. _____

3. _____

How to Make Your Own
Fortune Cookie

I've given up looking for a boyfriend. That's not to say
I won't be interested if the right guy comes along.
—Emily VanCamp

Shallow men believe in luck or in circumstances.
Strong men believe in cause and effect.
—Ralph Waldo Emerson

There's this neat paradox to life: we need to be clear about what we want but simultaneously let go of our attachment to its outcome. And there's evidence everywhere we look to support this paradox:

- You're running late to get somewhere and every possible obstacle seems to come your way.
- A husband fears his wife will leave him and then she actually does.
- A woman/man articulates her/his personal life all over social media and yet feels isolated and alone.
- A college student pursues happiness only to find herself anxious and stressed.
- The more technology advances and makes our lives easier, the more complex and challenging life seems to grow.
- The more choices we have, the less happy we seem to be.

The Universe, Nature—it all flows. There's no stopping the sun from rising each morning or preventing an ocean from ebbing and flooding. When we are living in the flow, happiness becomes the by-product.

But we humans so often try to stop that natural flow. We ignore our bodies when we are tired, guzzling caffeinated beverages a handful of hours before bed and then wondering why we can't fall asleep; we control our bodies with birth control pills for years and then grow frustrated with our bodies when we go off of them and find we aren't getting pregnant; we get nose jobs and tummy tucks, face-lifts and eye-lifts and wonder why we still struggle with self-esteem; we starve ourselves, depriving our bodies of nutrients (spiritually, physically, and emotionally) and then hate ourselves for giving into our very nature by eating or drinking in binge-worthy amounts.

Elizabeth Gilbert, author of *Big Magic,* refers to the paradox of creativity that can be applied to the push and pull we feel with our intimate relationships:

> The paradox that you need to comfortably inhabit, if you wish to live a contented creative life, goes something like this: "My creative expression must be the most important thing in the world to me (if I am to live artistically), and also not matter at all (if I am to live sanely)."[10]

So if we were to apply Gilbert's ingenious intellectual deduction to our intimate relationships, it would look something like this:

> The paradox that we need to comfortably inhabit, if we wish to live a contented life, goes something like

10   Elizabeth Gilbert, *Big Magic: Creative Living Beyond Fear* (New York: Riverhead Books, 2016), 135.

this: "My desire for a healthy, dynamic, rewarding, and authentic intimate relationship must be the most important thing in the world to me, and it also must not matter at all."

It's crazy, right? We do all of this inner reflection work, stay cognizant about those clandestine ARODs lurking around, clean and scour our metaphorical fridges, fill them with nutrient-packed relationships, follow those eight steps (while keeping those knickers on in those instances when we know it's much better than removing them). And yet we need to surrender and let go of expected, highly desired outcomes?

Yup.

There are no guarantees—whether in life or relationships. We can do all the right things and still end up without a rewarding, intimate relationship. But just like a river needs to flow downstream, we need to accept our own "currents," allowing things to happen *while simultaneously trying our best.* It's when we try to force that river to go upstream, against its natural flow, that we experience everything from exhaustion to anger.

The real fortune cookie of relationships is not found in the mass-produced pithy words printed inside the famous bent wafer any more than through a one-night stand. The mysterious, ephemeral dessert of intimate relationships is found through effort, an open heart and mind, and the tenacity of spirit to surrender to what has yet to manifest.

My friend Maggie had a negative experience dating a man she was serious with in her mid-thirties. It was so bad that she never wants to talk about it and is terrified to ever date again. She is now in her mid-fifties, enjoying her life but articulating in most of our conversations that she is lonely and would like to meet someone. Yet she refuses to go online, into a bar, or on a blind date set up by friends.

Maggie isn't making an effort. Cracking open a fortune cookie often necessitates effort.

My friend Anjie still continues to talk daily with her abusive father. She allows him to put her down, blaming his daughter for her second failed marriage. While it helps that she's left her abusive husband, until she addresses her father's abuse, it is unlikely that she will begin to heal and create the emotional and spiritual space necessary for a healthy intimate relationship.

Anjie is lonelier than ever these days, licking her wounds from her broken marriage. Her fortune cookie involves surrendering and self-reflection.

Everyone's fortune cookie looks different just as everyone's story is unique. The key is to accept wherever we are in our relationship journey, regularly filling ourselves with nutrient-packed habits and choices. There will be times in our journey when, try as we might, our fortune cookie is not producing what we believe we deserve or want. It is at that moment we must remember that we can't see the entire tapestry of our lives; we must remind ourselves that we have no idea what rewarding and fulfilling fortune is waiting for us in the near future.

Fortune or luck is a contradictory by-product of effort and letting go, of playful trying, of tenacity and ease.

Journal Time

Take a moment to write a letter to the Universe about what kind of intimate relationship you would like to experience. This can be with someone you are currently with or someone you have yet to meet. There is no wrong or right way to express what you want, though perhaps the more specific the better. When you are finished, read it aloud with conviction, as if the Universe is listening (as the Universe truly is). It is important to close the letter with a genuine thank you, articulating gratitude for what is on its way.

Then surrender, letting your wish out into the cosmos, accepting that the content of your letter has already been fulfilled.

Dear Universe,

_____

_____

_____

_____

_____

_____

_____

Diet Coke Denial

*It all comes down to one word...the F-bomb...it's really not
expressing how you really feel...it's sort of a cheap shot
to take...I'm talking about the word FINE...feeling like
roommates with your spouse, you're fine? You haven't had
sex in four months, you're fine? Really?? I don't think so.*
—Mel Robbins, Relationship Expert at TEDx Talk

One of my colleagues frequently complains about her thighs chafing whenever she wears shorts or skirts in the summer. She blames it on the intense heat and humidity in Southwest Houston while downing a Diet Coke almost every day at lunch. But just like the Diet Coke doesn't stave off her need for proper nutrition, her regular scapegoating of high temperatures does nothing to address the issue of her inner thighs rubbing against each other when she walks. Blaming the heat enables her to continue consuming the brown bubbly aspartame instead of considering why she typically finishes her meal with a Krispy Kreme donut. Blaming the heat renders her body a mere victim, allowing her to indulge in the world of pseudo nutrition.

While the jury is still out on whether aspartame is dangerous for us, the metaphor to the caramel-colored beverage (the caramel color has been definitively linked with cancer) still applies in cultivating healthy relationships. When we accept pseudo calories in place of the real thing, we are physically, spiritually, and psychologically starving ourselves. We deserve to experience authentic relationships, and that can only happen when we strip ourselves of one of the biggest caloric lies we tell ourselves: I'm fine.

Relationship expert and author Mel Robbins explains that "it's actually genius" on our part when we articulate to ourselves and others that we are fine, as then we can remain in our Diet Coke Land of Denial and not have to push ourselves to get out of our comfort zones and "actually do something" about the fact that we're not fine.

Fear is the cancer-causing caramel-colored source of our denial and blame. Fear prevents us from challenging ourselves. Fear offers a calorically empty feast of pseudo "fineness" that only perpetuates a cycle of frustration, settling, and self-sabotaging behaviors.

The other day, I treated myself to a pedicure. The woman pampering my feet asked me if I had any upcoming travel plans.

> **Me:** I'm heading home to New York.
> **Woman:** Oh, I'm from New York, too! I miss it. I wish I could go back, but my boyfriend won't let me.
> **Me:** (With great effort, I conceal my utter shock and frustration with her boyfriend.) Why not?
> **Woman:** (Flashes a sheepish smile.) My ex-boyfriend lives there. He doesn't want me seeing him.
> **Me:** What do *you* want to do?
> **Woman:** (Giggles uneasily.) I want to go. My boyfriend said he will decide if we can ever go.

I don't know if this woman still had a "thing" for her ex-boyfriend or if her current boyfriend was purely a control freak within their relationship. The backstory doesn't matter here. What does matter? The woman *wants* to go to New

York. She *misses* New York. Yet she is allowing someone outside of herself to determine whether she ever visits the Big Apple again. The woman's giggle was nothing more than a symptom of her fear, equivalent to "fine."

Married couples can fall prey to the sickly sweet F-bomb as much as singletons. My friend Betsy, a stay-at-home mom who has been married for fourteen years, recently opened up the following dialogue with me:

> **Betsy:** Sher, do you think it's enough that Martin (her husband) gives me $xxx a week budget to spend?
>
> **Me:** I think you're asking the wrong question. I think you need to ask yourself a different question: Do you think your husband should even be putting you on an allowance?
>
> [Insert BIG pause]
>
> **Betsy:** (quietly) Yeah, I have thought about that. But Martin's always been like that about money. It's okay. It doesn't really bother me.

Those words echoed in my head: *It doesn't really bother me.* What would it take for Betsy to get really bothered? How many cans of Diet Coke Denial does she need to swallow until she can be emotionally numb with "fineness"?

Betsy, like many of us, doesn't want to have "that" conversation, doesn't want to examine the ingredients in her Diet Coke Denial because it means she will need to step outside of her comfort zone. A conversation with Martin means admitting that buying the Costco-sized Diet Cokes is not a healthy choice; it means choosing an alternative. What are they going to do about it now? Addressing the taboo topic of budgets with the man she exchanged vows with means giving up the illusion of control. After all, Betsy can speak from her heart but can't determine the way Martin will take her words.

So Betsy never broaches the I'm-a-grown-woman-and-the-mother-of-your-children-and-therefore-find-being-on-an-allowance-disguised-as-a-budget-both-controlling-and-demeaning subject. She remains in her Diet Coke of Denial, where each figurative glass of brown bubbly leaves an increasingly bitter aftertaste in her mouth as she forms the paralyzing word: FINE.

To reiterate, singletons can fall prey to Diet Coke Denial just as easily as their committed contemporaries. I was (until recently) one myself.

Neil and I have remained friends throughout the writing of this book. But just as you can't be a little pregnant or regress in a pregnancy, once we had ventured into Intimacy Territory, Neil and I had a difficult time remaining in the Friend Zone. Every time we met, we both wanted more, but only one of us (*moi*) was open to exploring that possibility. Neil wanted to remain friends due to our geographic distance.

And for the past couple of years we were friends…with benefits. Neil would join me in the Diet Coke of Denial by saying, "No, we are so much more than Friends with Benefits." I could hear the wheels working overtime in his head to rationalize our behavior. "We're Benefits with Friends."

When you're in love with someone, when you're physically aching for this person, you are not thinking straight. It's beer-goggles-meets-Shallow-Hal on steroids. It's like, "Hm, that makes absolutely no sense and pisses me off that you aren't being authentic, but man I just want to kiss you right now."

So we indulged, devouring empty calories with pleasure (rendering our attachment even more unhealthy). And then we would stop and promise ourselves we would just remain friends—no benefits.

But the platonic nature of our relationship just never lasted. We did the Diet Coke Denial Dance until we were swollen with empty calories of resentment, anguish, and frustration. Our relationship was no different than any other intimate relationship: it needed to flourish or be laid to rest. It could no longer remain in the fabricated world of "fineness" that was growing more gossamer each day.

Like a drug addict, I was hooked on Neil, and it wasn't good for our physical, emotional, or spiritual health. Regardless of the many red flags and verbal alterations we created (e.g., avoiding the words *girlfriend* and *boyfriend*; convincing ourselves that our relationship was beyond mere labels, etc.), I knew deep down it was time to lovingly kick all those Diet Coke cans to the recycling bin and bid farewell to the nutritional nightmare of us.

Yet I still didn't *want* to give up my codependent relationship. True, I was receiving emotional crumbs, but what would I do without those precious crumbs?

I asked the Universe for guidance, and within hours it came in the form of Mel Robbins's TEDx Talk called "How to Stop Screwing Yourself Over." I'm sure the Universe had offered multiple opportunities to help me leave the saccharine-sweet world of relationship "Fineness," but until Robbins's TEDx Talk magically popped up onto my computer screen (I hadn't even been on YouTube!), I hadn't been hungry enough to notice or digest the lesson necessary for my growth.

> Physical force is required to change your behavior. Do you think that someone who wants to lose weight ever feels like going on a diet? Of course not! Do you think they ever feel like eating boiled chicken and peas instead of a croissant? I don't think so! You're so damn busy waiting to feel like it and you're never going to…. You have to force yourself (and I mean force)…. Any break from your routine will require force…. When we feel stuck or dissatisfied in life, it is a signal…one of your most basic human needs is not being met.[11]

So Neil and I had both felt "stuck"—our Yellow Dye #5 "Friendship" was rendering us sick, unable to move forward. We were both attached to each other's crumbs, both settling for less than we deserved just so we could experience another dopamine hit of the other's company. We were never going to *not* want to experience that hit. We were too entrenched in our unhealthy relationship to admit the ever-growing caloric toxicity.

The common side effects of giving up diet sodas (more specifically, aspartame) are anxiety, appetite changes, difficulty concentrating, cravings, dizziness, fatigue, headaches, insomnia, restlessness, and weight changes. Saying goodbye to Neil, deleting all personal cyber footprints of him, and donating his gifts and sentimental cards came with a similar string of side effects. I craved the sound of his voice, ached for the feel of his skin against mine, and hungered for the

11   Mel Robbins, "How to Stop Screwing Yourself Over," June 11, 2011, TEDx, https://www.youtube.com/watch?v=Lp7E973zozc.

sight of his eyes mischievously looking into mine. I felt tremors of anxiety when I knew I couldn't reach for the phone and ask for his advice about something like I had for the past two years. I sat with the ghost of our relationship in my car, my home, my town.

Benefits with Friends my ass. I had fallen in love with Neil, and it took nothing short of a Herculean effort to physically force myself to remain in the Land of Hangover Neil, never allowing myself to give in and reach out to my drug of choice.

Like an addiction to any drug, mine took its sweet time to leave my system. Each day, thanks to Mel Robbins's words of tough love, I reminded myself that I was sitting through the painful withdrawal of Hangover Neil because I *knew* I needed to be free of him.

After several months sans Neil, I noticed little rays of nutrients lighting my path, letting me know that the emotional storm of withdrawal was finally beginning to wane: I went hours without thinking about Neil, I grew busy with family and friends, and as new men entered my life, I gave them a real chance in ways I probably wouldn't have done with Neil in the picture. I also noticed that I was growing stronger, stronger than I ever was eating the codependent crumbs dished out by my friendship with Neil.

More months passed and I began to find myself seeing past dialogues with Neil in a clearer light. Neil had genuinely loved me *as much as he could*, but I would never be a priority for him. He was too consumed with his own inner battles to be more than a friend. We had both shown weakness in accepting slices of confectionary affection that rendered us bloated with dissatisfaction.

Facing my Denial Diet Coke of "Fineness" was equal parts pain and anxiety, but that force, that taking responsibility for what I wanted *in the end*, keeping my eye on the true dessert (emotional, spiritual, and physical freedom) was worth every heart-wrenching moment.

Fear is not the only form of denial. It can arrive in the form of its sibling: blame. When we blame ourselves or someone else for a failing relationship, we are merely creating a clever excuse to remain in artificial sweetener "Fineness." Neil and I shared the responsibility for our Denial Dance. Both of us received crumbs and pushed aside frustrations and dissatisfactions in order to keep the caloric mess of us intact.

It is only when we remove our Diet Coke goggles of denial that we can begin to take responsibility for our role in a relationship; it is only then that we can leave our comfort zones, recycling "Fineness" to make space for flourishing.

Journal Time

Take a moment to identify something you *want* to experience in your relationship—either with yourself or someone else.

_____

_____

_____

_____

_____

_____

What is keeping you in Diet Coke Denial Land or in a perpetual state of "Fineness"? What fear is keeping you in your comfort zone?

_____

_____

_____

_____

_____

_____

Physical force brings change. What five things could you physically force yourself to do today to get past your comfort-zone Fineness into a nutrient-dense world where you can achieve the desires you listed above?

1. _____

_____

2. _____

_____

3. _____

_____

4. _____

_____

5. _____

_____

Why You'll Never Starve on the Friendship Diet

One cannot think well, love well, sleep
well, if one has not dined well.
—Virginia Woolf, *A Room of One's Own*

Paradoxically, I've found that loving myself is
the only way to get where I'm going.
—Author and screenwriter Tracy McMillan ("The
Person You Really Need to Marry" TEDx)

I was twelve years old when Hurricane Gloria hit our Long Island town. Overnight, we lost electricity and the ability to navigate our cars on the flooded streets strewn with trees. The Category 4 storm rendered us without phone service and left a rapidly thawing refrigerator in its wake.

Nevertheless, the fall of 1985 was one of the most rewarding, fulfilling times of my childhood. The 100+ mph winds may have wreaked havoc on our lives, but it also created a physical force that brought my family and friends together. My father made a makeshift stove outside from our coal grill, firing up hamburgers and hot dogs for our family and neighbors to eat. Friends came by from the neighborhood with bags of marshmallows in tow. Our backyard morphed into an enchanted forest as we searched for the perfect fallen tree branch to heat up the white puffs of confectionary heaven. Without the background of the normally omnipresent television or the beeping microwave, we were forced to slow down and connect. As we told ghost stories and played board games by candlelight, our laughter was clearer and sounded fuller without modern-day distractions standing in the way.

It is our perception that creates our reality. My reality that late autumn in 1985 was one of decadent slowness, an Indian summer of childhood where we played hopscotch and ate peanut butter sandwiches that tasted like manna for one last time before adolescence encroached. It was Mother Nature treating us to days off from school and a magical landscape of debris to explore and uncover.

My mother's reality was an altogether different one. She had recently lost her mother. While she was physically there for my sisters and me, her soul was in mourning, floating far above the debris and devastation of Smithtown, New York, to commune with her personal cracks and fissures.

Yet while my mother and I (and perhaps everyone affected by Hurricane Gloria) experienced very different realities, neither of us was starving. Starving in relationships can only occur by choice. My mother made a choice to stay outside and help my father hand out those burgers and hotdogs. She made a choice to help the younger, less coordinated kids in the neighborhood adhere Jett-Puffed delicacies to their broken tree branches. She made a choice to bring my sisters and me peanut butter sandwiches while we played another round of checkers by candlelight.

A relationship is defined by the way two or more concepts, objects, or people are connected. This life we live is all about our relationships. When we nurture our relationships, we are nurturing ourselves.

The days after Hurricane Gloria were a time of wonder and fulfillment for me because, despite the turbulent weather conditions, I was surrounded by people I loved. The way our neighbors and friends *related* to each other sustained me, enriched me, nourished me more when the distractions of everyday life went dormant.

And while my mother mourned her relationship with my grandmother, it didn't prevent her from experiencing nourishment from family and friends during the storm of her inner and outer world.

Thankfully, we don't need a hurricane to wake up and appreciate the relationships we have. And we certainly don't need to be in an intimate relationship with someone else to appreciate the most important relationship in the world: the one with ourselves. Tracy McMillan (screenwriter for *Mad Men*) refers to a realization she had on a date:

> I went on a first date. And about 30 minutes into the date, I found myself paying attention not to whether he liked me, but how I felt in his presence....I am more interested in how I feel about me than how he feels about me.[12]

Tracy McMillan will never starve. Her Friendship Diet is founded on a commitment to herself—not because she is selfish but because she's realized an all-important truth: our most important emotional nutrition needs to come from our relationship with ourselves.

Young girls fall prey to neglecting or not even considering their relationship with themselves. One of my

12   Pangambam S, "Tracy McMillan on The Person You Really Need to Marry," The Singju Post, March 31, 2016, https://singjupost .com/tracy-mcmillan-on-the-person-you-really-need-to-marry-full -transcript/2/?singlepage=1l.

middle school students came rushing into my classroom after school with tears in her eyes. Her best friend liked this boy and asked him to the school dance. The boy agreed, then met my student and asked her to the dance.

Looking at me in panic, she said, "What should I do? I'm so confused!"

It didn't matter that my student had been best friends with her girlfriend since the first grade; it didn't matter whether she even liked this boy; the frustration and confusion she articulated stemmed purely from one source: neglecting the relationship with herself.

When we neglect our relationship with ourselves, we are nutritionally starving ourselves, falling off the Friendship Diet wagon and giving full reign and power to others. Nothing good will ever come from authorizing our power to someone else. It is a prescription for emotional dissatisfaction and a hunger that never satisfies.

We are ever-changing, and so our inner world will always offer us ripe opportunities for self-reflection and action. It is impossible to starve when we acknowledge and cultivate the never-ending smorgasbord of who we are and what we are becoming. Regardless of our external circumstances, our spiritual bellies will always be full when we accept and embrace ourselves. When we remove the comforting fat of denial and build a dish made of authenticity and kindness—always beginning with ourselves first—we will never experience emotional malnutrition.

I'm so proud of you for joining the Friendship Diet wagon! It takes courage to try something new, to take action and create a recipe that's all your own.

Thank You for Reading

While this book has come to a close, your journey through the Friendship Diet is just beginning! Sign up on my blog below to be notified of any pending book releases or updated content.

What are you waiting for?

Sign up now: www.sheri-jacobs.com/book-bonus

Please do not hesitate to connect with me if you have any questions or feedback about *The Friendship Diet*. Relationships truly possess the capacity to feed or starve us. It is up to each of us to commit to a journey of self-awareness in order to discover what qualities in ourselves and others fuel or deplete personal relationships—including the most important one we will ever experience: the one with ourselves.

I would be happy to hear from you, and I enjoy connecting with readers.

Thanks again,

Sheri Jacobs

A Quick Favor Please?

Before you go, can I ask you for a quick favor?

Good, I knew I could count on you.

Would you please leave this book a review on Amazon?

Reviews are very important for authors, as they help us sell more books, which in turn enables me to write more books for you!

Please take a quick minute to go to Amazon and leave this book an honest review. I promise it doesn't take long, but it can help me reach more readers just like you.

Thank you for reading, and thank you so much for being part of the journey.

Sheri Jacobs

About the Author

Sheri Jacobs is the published author of *Dream Write* (pen name Kiss), a children's book that uses humor and creativity to help transform a fearful state into an empowering one. She was a two-time finalist in THEMA'S short story contest and received Honorable Mention for a short story at Glimmer Train Literary (top 3% out of 1,000 submissions). She is a full-time teacher to middle school students, a professional voice-over artist, and a commercial and theater actress. Sheri uses her gift for public speaking and comedic storytelling to help motivate men and women to create their own diet for rewarding relationships. Learn more at www.sheri-jacobs.com.

www.ingramcontent.com/pod-product-compliance
Lightning Source LLC
Chambersburg PA
CBHW070808280326
41934CB00012B/3115